A.L. BURRUSS
THE LIFE OF A GEORGIA POLITICIAN AND A
MAN TO TRUST

*For Ken Nix
a fellow legislator who served
with Al*

A.L. BURRUSS
THE LIFE OF A GEORGIA POLITICIAN AND A
MAN TO TRUST

by
MARGARET BENNETT WALTERS

Margaret B. Walters

Kennesaw State University Press

The Kennesaw State University Press
Kennesaw, Georgia USA

Copyright © 2009 The Kennesaw State University Press.

All rights reserved. No part of this book may be used or reproduced in any manner without prior written consent of the publisher.

The Kennesaw State University Press, Kennesaw, GA
www.kennesaw.edu/ksupress

Author: Margaret Bennett Walters
Editor: Cathleen Salsburg-Pfund
Acquisitions Editor: Laura Dabundo
Cover & Book Design: Holly S. Miller

The photographs, brochures, and letters appearing in this book are part of the Burruss family collection and have been used with permission from the family.

Library of Congress Cataloging-in-Publication Data

Walters, Margaret Bennett, 1950-
A. L. Burruss: The Life of a Georgia Politician and a Man to Trust p. cm.
Includes bibliographical references and index.
ISBN 978-1-933483-18-4
1. Burruss, A. L., 1927-1986. 2. Legislators--Georgia--Biography. 3. Georgia. General Assembly. House of Representatives--Biography. 4. Georgia--Politics and government--1951- I. Title.
F291.3.B87W35 2009
328.758092--dc22 [B]
2009023212

Published in 2011
Printed in the United States of America

10 9 8 7 6 5 4 3 2

Paper meets ANSI and library standards for archival quality.

For my husband, Steve, and my daughter, Jacqueline.

Contents

Foreword ... ix

Chapter 1 ... 1
Introduction: "A Simple Chicken Plucker"

Chapter 2 ... 15
Ambition and Avocation: Burruss Enters Public Service

Chapter 3 ... 31
State Representative A. L. Burruss:
The Early Years, 1970–1976

Chapter 4 ... 63
The Senior Statesman: In His Element

Chapter 5 ... 81
Conclusion: A. L. Burruss, July 3, 1927–May 10, 1986

A. L. Burruss Chronology ... 91

Appendix A ... 95
Transcript of A. L. Burruss Lenten Lift Lunch Speech,
March 26, 1986

Appendix B ... 97
A. L. Burruss Institute of Public Service & Research

Notes ... 99

Select Bibliography ... 109

Index ... 111

Illustrations and Photographs follow page 41

Foreword

A. L. Burruss established his business, served on the county commission, and rose to prominence in the General Assembly during a golden age of Cobb County's history. The arrival of the aircraft industry during World War II triggered Cobb's population explosion. As cotton fields turned into subdivisions, the county experienced unprecedented prosperity. The role of the politician in this era of rapid growth was to build the infrastructure necessary to sustain a high quality of life. Burruss and his generation of remarkable statesmen seemed uniquely qualified to do just that.

Cobb County, Georgia was blessed throughout the late twentieth century by a succession of gifted leaders who found creative ways of serving local needs. As Margaret Walters points out, A. L. Burruss came from relatively humble origins and was not a Cobb countian by birth. But he arrived at a time when opportunity abounded for imaginative, hard-working young people. With his best friend, Chet Austin, he built Tip Top Poultry into a highly successful business. Then, he turned to politics, winning an election in 1964 to Cobb's first five-member county commission. After a term on the commission, he won a seat in the Georgia House of Representatives, which he held until his death in 1986. During the 1970s and 1980s A. L. Burruss and his colleague Joe Mack Wilson dominated the local legislative delegation and funneled state dollars to Cobb County for a host of worthwhile local projects.

Among his many contributions, Burruss proved to be a great friend of higher education. His name is properly enshrined at Kennesaw State University in the A. L. Burruss Business Building and the A. L. Burruss Institute of Public Service & Research. We can all be grateful that the Burruss Institute saw the need for a book-length biography and that Professor Walters was chosen to take on the task. Now, we have a work that will remind future generations of A. L. Burruss's distinguished service and will challenge us all to emulate the virtues of honor and integrity that were the hallmarks of his career.

Thomas A. Scott
Professor Emeritus of History
Kennesaw State University

Acknowledgments

I owe grateful thanks for the genesis of this project to Carol Pierannunzi, former director of the A. L. Burruss Institute of Public Service & Research, and to Laura Dabundo, former director of The Kennesaw State University Press and professor of English at Kennesaw State University, for commissioning me to undertake this biography of A. L. Burruss. It has been one of the greatest pleasures of my scholarly life to discover this legendary Georgia politician. To these two I also owe appreciation for their helpful comments, Carol as a reader of the manuscript and Laura as the initial editor. I am also thankful to the Burruss Institute for course release time from teaching to research and write this book. I am also deeply indebted to Thomas Allan Scott, professor emeritus of History at Kennesaw State University, for reading and commenting on the manuscript and sharing with me his deep knowledge of the history of Cobb County and Burruss's place in it. My thanks also go to Albert Nason, archivist at the Jimmy Carter Library and Museum in Atlanta, Georgia, for helping me locate materials related to Burruss's involvement in policy while Carter was president.

My thanks also go to the interns from Kennesaw State University and The Kennesaw State University Press: Jonae Jackson, Jessica Obenschein, Melissa Stiers, and Leah Hale, who helped with research and fact checking. Stephanie Renz prepared transcripts of several interviews. LaRondra West was especially helpful in fact checking, compiling the bibliography, and creating an early version of the index. I am grateful to all the interns for their keen interest and valuable assistance in preparing this book for publication. I also wish to thank Cathleen Salsburg-Pfund, the editor of the final draft of this manuscript.

I would be remiss not to mention my friends and colleagues who listened to me talk ad infinitum about Burruss and who encouraged me along the way—Anne Richards, Martha Bowden, Laura Dabundo, Beth Danielle, Mike Tierce, Michelle Medved, Bill Rice, Jim Elledge, Susan Hunter, and my other colleagues in the Department of English at Kennesaw State University.

In addition to the early readers of my manuscript, I am very grateful to those who knew A. L. Burruss personally and let me interview them. In particular Burruss's immediate family—wife Bobbi Burruss and his children Renée Burruss Davis and Robin Burruss—were warm and welcoming and their insight into Al formed a portrait of him as loving husband and father. The Burruss family also generously shared many of the photographs that appear in this book. Several of Burruss's siblings were also very helpful in sharing with me many warm memories and anecdotes about their brother—my thanks go to Linda Moore, Jane Ragan, Gerald Burruss, and Buddy Burruss. I am thankful to Chet Austin, Al's lifelong friend, for sharing his account of their friendship and long business partnership at Tip Top Poultry. My thanks also go to those friends and political colleagues who shared their stories of Al with me—former Governor Roy E. Barnes, former State Legislator Terry Lawler, and Al's former pastor and friend, Reverend Charles Sineath, retired minister of the First United Methodist Church of Marietta. A longtime legislative aide, who wished to remain anonymous, was also a great help.

I am most grateful to my family. This book could not have been written without the love, encouragement, and support of my husband, Steve Walters, and my daughter, Jacqueline Walters.

CHAPTER 1

INTRODUCTION: "A SIMPLE CHICKEN PLUCKER"

A. L. Burruss often referred to himself as a "simple chicken plucker."[1] A self effacing man who loved his family and friends and was a lifelong supporter of Georgia's citizens and especially the people of Cobb County, Burruss always saw himself as one of the common people, albeit one who was fortunate enough to be successful at most anything he put his hand to, be it business or politics. Al Burruss acquired Tip Top Poultry, Inc., a chicken-processing plant located in Marietta, Georgia, in the early 1950s and turned it into a highly successful company, one of several he came to own, in the process. Well liked and respected by all who met him and dealt with him in his businesses, Burruss found it a natural next step to move into public service. Burruss began a new phase in his life in 1964 when he was elected one of the five commissioners in Cobb County's newly formed five-member county commission.[2] He served as a Cobb County commissioner from 1965 to 1969. In 1968, Burruss was elected to the Georgia House of Representatives, where he served from 1969 until his death in 1986. He was greatly mourned at his untimely death from cancer, and hundreds attended his funeral, including former President Jimmy Carter. The two men had been close friends since Carter's first campaign for governor of Georgia in 1966 when Burruss had flown him around the state in his plane.

The story of how a simple chicken-plucker became a highly respected and honored elder statesman is essentially an American success story of the twentieth century, with all the elements of such a story: an aggressive drive to succeed; a willingness to work hard; perseverance in overcoming obstacles; an understanding of people, how to win friends, and convert antagonists to supporters; and the knowlegdge of how to manage a company, including its money and its people.Burruss was guided by his faith in God and thankfulness for all the blessings he felt were bestowed on him.

Governor Roy Barnes said of his close friend and longtime colleague in the Georgia Assembly: "Al is the epitome of the American Dream, someone who came from very humble beginnings, worked hard, was eternally optimistic, and then decided to give back. That's the full cycle of the American Dream."[3] Going into politics, says his brother Buddy Burruss, fulfilled Burruss's desire to help people where he thought he could really make a difference. Burruss's sister Jane Ragan remembers her brother's interest in politics as the result of his seeing something wrong and thinking he could make it right, make it better. Of her husband's political career, Bobbi Burruss, his wife of thirty-seven years, notes that her husband "never forgot where he came from" and continued to run for public office "because it was a way to help people."[4] His daughter Renée Burruss Davis concurs that her father never sought political office for personal aggrandizement, but saw it only as a way to help others: "he was always there to help people," she says.[5]

A. L. Burruss was born on July 3, 1927, in rural Forsyth County, the son of carpenter John Chesley Burruss[6] and his wife Eula Malinda Corn.[7] Bobbi Burruss relates an amusing family anecdote about her husband's birth date. Burruss's mother used to say that because she had him on July 3, they had to take the next day off to celebrate.[8] Though he was called "Al" most of his life, it was only a nickname. Burruss was only given the initials "A. L." Bobbi Burruss recalls the story that Al's mother wanted to name him after his two grandfathers but didn't like her choices—Albert, Luke, Alfred, or Luther, so decided to give him the initials A. L. instead. It's unusual that as the eldest of eleven children—Sarah, Betty, Jimmie, Shirley (who died at fourteen months of age), Peggy, Buddy, Gerald, Linda, Jane, and Dan—that A. L. was the only one not given a name. According to his wife, he was never happy with being called Al though that's how he was known from the time he got out of high school until his death.[9] Burruss's sister, Linda Moore, recalls that when she asked her mother how to spell her brother's name, her mother would say, "His name is A period, L period, that's his name."[10] Though Burruss was known as Al to Bobbi and most of his friends, as well as to his fellow politicians and constituents, many in his immediate family continued to call him by the initials he grew up with, A. L., some even to this day.

Legendary Atlanta reporter Celestine Sibley, who wrote about Burruss for *The Atlanta Journal and Constitution*, interviewed Burruss about his early beginnings. He told her he "came from the hills of Forsyth County—Hopewell Community, out from Silver City, out from Cumming" and the family moved to Smyrna when he was seven or eight years old, where his father got a job as a carpenter and painter.[11] Times were hard for the Burrusses, just as they were for many Americans during the Great Depression. He reserved his highest praise for his mother, explaining to Sibley that it was "the tenacity and dedication of his mother, who kept the family together." Of his youth, Burruss recalled that "his summers were the happiest [...] because he spent many of them in Forsyth County on the farm of his grandfather, Luke Burruss."[12] In what he says of his grandfather can be seen the seeds of his own character; Burruss noted that his grandfather "was everything I ever wanted to be—hard working, honest, full of determination that's hard to find these days."[13] The qualities he so admired about his grandfather—that he was hard-working, honest, and full of determination—were the hallmarks of Burruss's own approach to life.

Chet Austin, who was Al's closest friend, met him in the third grade after the Burruss family moved to Smyrna. The two were recess partners and playmates, then partnered as teens in various jobs around Smyrna.[14] Austin recalls that his friend worked all the time as he was growing up—mowing lawns, doing odd jobs, and working as a janitor while he was in high school; and Austin joined Burruss in many of these occupations. Even while in elementary school, Al worked as a delivery boy and on a farm.[15] As Burruss told Celestine Sibley, he was helped by the principal of Smyrna High School, who was aware that Al needed to work so he could stay in high school, so he arranged for Burruss and Austin to substitute for the janitor. This was during World War II, when it was hard to find anyone to take that job because of the shortage of manpower.[16] As Austin explains, the high school's custodian was a tenant farmer who had to leave to tend his crops during the spring gathering season, so the two young men took over his job.[17] For several years, he and Burruss arrived early to fire up the coal-fueled furnace and stayed after school to clean up. Additionally, the two cleaned local Baptist and Methodist churches, of which Austin remarks that "We got pretty good at it."[18]

Once Burruss and Austin graduated from Smyrna High School, in 1944, Austin went on to Georgia Military College in Milledgeville. Burruss, who could not afford college, went to work. In later years, Al always explained that instead of going to college, he "went to the school of hard knocks."[19] During the year Austin was away at college, Burruss continued to work multiple jobs. At one point, he was "a bicycle-riding mail clerk at Bell Aircraft in Marietta,"[20] and he also worked at Graves Refrigeration.[21] Yet, his friendship with Austin was important to him, and Burruss kept close to Austin even after he left for college. When Austin returned home for winter break, he worked several weeks with Burruss at Graves, even though he says he had little knowledge of what he was doing. But Burruss, he says, was smart and could grasp things.[22] Both young men, however, were eager to join in the war effort. Since neither was yet eighteen years of age, enlisting for military service required parental consent.

Burruss was the first to get his parents' consent and in 1945, shortly before his eighteenth birthday, he joined the US Naval Reserve. Celestine Sibley points out that "the war ended just as [Burruss] finished boot camp and headed for the Pacific, halting him in the Philippines."[23] He served as a refrigeration machinist in the Philippines, training he was to put to good use once he returned to Georgia. However, Burruss was unable to serve his full time in the Navy because his family had an urgent need for him to be at home and he was given an honorable discharge for hardship.[24] Austin, who had enlisted in the Navy in the fall of 1945, after obtaining parental consent shortly before his eighteenth birthday, was stationed in Hawaii when he received a telegram from his friend with the announcement, "Bobbi and I married."[25]

Bobbi Burruss, the former Barbara Nelle Elrod,[26] recalls that as soon as she met Al, she knew he was the man for her: "I met him through my best girlfriend. I got him a blind date with her. And then we decided we were going to get married. Just about that quick, too."[27] Burruss also recognized in her the woman he wanted to marry, and their courtship began in earnest, if only on the weekends. A friend of his had introduced him to flying and Burruss soon had his pilot's license and would borrow a friend's plane to go see her. She recalls that: "We just knew it from the moment, and he used to fly up. He was [working] in Smyrna, and I lived in Cornelia, Georgia. And he would fly up with one of his friends in a J-2 Cub, that's a tiny little airplane, and land in our friend's cow pasture. And we would have weekends and that would be it because he worked, of course."[28] The two married on August 17, 1947, and moved to Smyrna. They had two sons and a daughter: Robin Alan, born February 5,1952; Michael Adair, born April 16, 1955, who died in infancy; and Patricia Renée, born December 10, 1958.[29] In the early days of their marriage, Burruss ran his own refrigeration and service business in Smyrna, Georgia. It wasn't until the early 1950s that he acquired the company in which he would eventually make his fortune.

Fortuitously, Burruss met the owners of Tip Top Poultry, then located behind the YWCA in downtown Marietta, through his refrigeration business; they had contracted with him to build a walk-in freezer. At that time, Tip Top was owned by two partners, E. T. Banks and Vernon Green. Banks liked Burruss and, wanting to retire, decided to sell him his share in the partnership. Because Burruss had no means of buying him out, Banks offered to finance his purchase of the partnership. Suspicious of the deal, Green insisted the two buy him out as well. Though Banks didn't want to do so, he bought his old partner out in a limited partnership because he was eager to quit the business. Thus, Burruss acquired Tip Top Poultry and became its president in 1951 shortly before his son Robin was born.[30]

Around this same time, Austin, who had gone to work at Lockheed after returning from the war, began courting his future wife, Hazel, who also worked at Lockheed. Austin recounts how he took Hazel to meet Al and Bobbi one night. At the time the Burrusses were living in Smyrna, which was considered rural country. In 1950, Smyrna's population was only 2,005;[31] and the current Atlanta Road was the main highway, then known as the Dixie Highway.[32]

Finding the house dark, the Austins decided to wait though this made Hazel nervous. But when she met Burruss, Austin says, she loved him. The couples became friends, just as the men had always been, and it wasn't long before they found themselves sitting around the dining table, coming up with a plan for bringing Austin into the chicken processing business with his friend. As Austin explains, Al was having to learn about and manage the business at the same time; he was working himself very hard and getting very little sleep. Sometimes they would go to his house and Burruss would be so tired he'd lie on the floor and immediately fall asleep.[33] In short order, Austin joined Burruss as a partner and owner of Tip Top Poultry. Their duties were split along their own inclinations and what they knew best. Burruss was the front man, the one who met with customers and worked with the community, and Austin was an administrator, taking care of payroll and the financial end of the business. Later, Burruss's brothers Jimmie and Buddy joined the company, too.

Al Burruss's personality in particular suited him for his role as front man at Tip Top Poultry and later at the state legislature. Those who knew him recall that he was always smiling; Austin contends that anyone who met him loved him. Though Burruss had his share of opposition in business and the legislature, his friends and family recall a man who had great strength of personality. Former Georgia Governor Barnes says that, "The force of Al Burruss' personality would have made him a center of influence in and of itself. But with the friendships and network that he built with President Carter (Governor Carter, then President Carter), Joe Frank Harris, the chairman of the appropriations committee, and with others gave him an inordinate amount of influence."[34]

During the period when he was a young married man and father and starting up his poultry business, Burruss also found spiritual strength in the friendships he made with three other couples. The young people were close friends and went to one another's house on Saturday nights, Austin says, because they couldn't afford to go anywhere else. Austin recalls the spiritual awakening of his friend:

> When we were young, and had only a few children between us four couples, we started attending a little Methodist church. Before that, Al didn't go to church. Bobbi's brother and his wife, Chet's cousin and her husband, Chet and Hazel,

> and Al and Bobbi started going and joined the church. But
> Al did it with more depth to him than the rest of us. He had
> a Paul's conversion; he felt it very, very strongly.[35]

Though his great-grandfather on his mother's side of the family had been a preacher, it wasn't until after the death of his infant son, Michael, that Burruss's spiritual faith grew. But as Austin and his family recall, Burruss never did anything halfway. He became one of the founding members of the Tillman Memorial Methodist Church in Smyrna, which now has a memorial garden in Burruss's name.

Al and Bobbi Burruss moved to Marietta in 1959, where they joined the First United Methodist Church of Marietta, a church in which he eventually served on the Administrative Board and Finance Committee[36] and became good friends with Reverend Charles Sineath, the minister. Rev. Sineath remembers Al Burruss for his extraordinary faith and spiritual wisdom.[37] When the church was planning a new family life hall, the original budget grew from $2.5 million to $3.2 million, and the Board thought it would not be able to build it as planned. During a meeting at which many ideas were being discussed, without any solutions being proposed, Burruss spoke up, making what Rev. Sineath calls an "affirmation of faith." Al framed the question in terms of how faith informed the committee's decision.

> Is this the building as the commission has planned it, the building God wants us to build? Do we believe it will be harder for God to give us $3.2 million than it would be for Him to give us $2.5 million? Well, if we believe this is the building God wants us to have and we believe He can provide, I'm going to believe we can build it and trust God and do it.

In Rev. Sineath's view, Burruss taught people to look at the question of God's stewardship in a new way, as a way to affirm their faith in the power of God, and that this way of thinking created excitement in the church. After Burruss's persuasive speech, the vote was unanimous in favor of the new building. Rev. Sineath points out that, despite initial misgivings, the church built the hall for $3.2 million and paid for it in three years. He also recalls Burruss's generosity in the mid-1970s when he anonymously donated part of the fee so people in the church who wanted to could attend an annual ministry known as Basic Life Lessons, aimed at Christians who wanted guidance in living their lives according to biblical tradition. Burruss had previously attended his ministry with his son Robin, and the experience had made a strong impression on them both, one he felt others would benefit from. Because he feared that young people just starting out in life could not afford the fee of $150, he agreed to cover half the cost, a plan Rev. Sineath says Burruss proposed himself, without prompting. When attendance from church members went up over one hundred, Rev. Sineath says he noticed the difference the ministry made in the life of the church, that "it changed the accent of the church," a difference he says Al Burruss made possible by his anonymous donation and his public endorsement of the ministry.[38]

As he was recovering from exploratory surgery in March of 1986, Burruss recorded a speech he had earlier promised to deliver for the Church's annual Lenten Lunch. Though the surgery had revealed Burruss had pancreatic cancer, he still felt compelled to speak to church members about his faith, even in the face of almost certain death. In his speech, one can see the strong faith that nurtured him throughout his life.

> Since the news has come that I have pancreatic cancer that is most probably terminal, I've been strangely calm and sustained. I give all the credit for this to the fact that my faith was there stronger than even I believed it to be. I am not panicked. It's true that I have spoke about the possibility that my life will be shorter than I want it to be. But I am also encouraged by the fact that my faith tells me that my death and my judgment days can be changed, but they can only be changed by our God and our Maker. [...] Please take this message home with you: God is real and He will be with us through any trial or tribulation that may come our way. I firmly believe that God is greater than any problems that we have. Please continue to remember to pray for me and my family. I thank you for listening and may God bless you.[39]

Chapter 1: Introduction: A Simple Chicken Plucker

Just as his faith was an important part of his life, so was his family. As his brother Buddy remembers it, though he was ten years younger than Burruss, the eldest brother worked hard to help his family while he was growing up and especially after he became successful. Though he may have seen it as his Christian duty to help his family, that he loved them very much is always in evidence. Buddy Burruss, who was born while his brother was still serving in the Philippines, remembers the family moving back and forth from Cobb county to Forsyth county, where the Corns lived, because his father had a hard time making a living for his large family.

Because the birth of the Burruss siblings spanned the years from Al's birth in 1927 until the birth of Dan, the youngest, in 1950, Al was considerably older than some of the youngest and served as something of a father figure for them. Linda Burruss Moore, born six years after Buddy, tells the story of how she was named after the Frank Sinatra song, "Linda," popular the year of her birth. Jane Burruss Ragan, born two years after Linda and nineteen years after A. L., remembers her older brother as a father figure and that he was very protective of her. She tells the story of how, when the two of them were working on George Busbee's campaign for Georgia governor, Burruss told her to keep their sibling relationship a secret until after the election. A. L. became Busbee's campaign manager after Busbee won the Democratic primary. Because Jane was working as a volunteer on the campaign, Burruss feared people might disparage her work as favoritism and he wished to protect her. After being elected governor, it was Busbee who told everyone about the connection. Busbee was so impressed with Ragan's work that he hired her as a secretary to one of his administrative assistants once he took office. Interestingly, though no one else knew they were brother and sister, Ragan says she "never heard a bad word about Al" from anyone the whole time they worked on the campaign.

Buddy Burruss, too, reports that A. L. "was a great brother; he'd do anything in the world he could for you," and, after working with him for many years at Tip Top, found him a "great boss." Even though Burruss was known for his generosity at the chicken processing plant, Buddy said he wouldn't agree to purchase new equipment unless a clear case was given for its need. This was also true for some, as Buddy refers to them, "down and out" people who asked Burruss for loans. However, Burruss always took his own council in such matters. Buddy recalls that his brother had made several loans to someone whom Buddy thought was a poor risk, and when Buddy told him so, Burruss told him it was none of his affair. His siblings were only too happy to repay him; later, when he ran for political office, they worked as volunteers in his political campaigns.

It was his mother, however, of all his family, to whom Burruss gave credit for holding the family together. On May 12, 1985, *The Marietta Daily Journal*'s Mother's Day tribute featured Eula Burruss and quotes A. L., who, in reply to the question of why his mother was so special, said:

> Other than my wife, my mother has had the greatest influence on my life. My mother and I went through some difficult times after the Depression. She always encouraged me to excel even though we had limited resources. She insisted that I go to school and made sure that I always had clean clothes. She was like the Rock of Gibraltar.[40]

Linda Moore remembers that her brother frequently called his mother from wherever he was—be it the State House or when he was on the road—to ask how she was doing, and he always referred to her as his "Rock of Gibraltar."

In the descriptions of what life with Burruss was like by his immediate family, the same attributes others knew him by—that he was hard working, determined, and generous—came through in their perceptions of him as a father and husband. According to Bobbi, her husband seemed to have more hours than anyone else because he always seemed to be able to do more than anyone else. According to Renée Davis, her father never missed a ball game or performance: "I cannot ever remember a time when he was not in the audience, and I was a very active teenager and young child. And I don't know how he did it because he had to have left some pretty big meetings to come to be wherever I was performing." She also remembers that mornings with her dad belonged to her and Robin, while he let their mother get more sleep. It was Burruss who prepared the kids' breakfast, got them ready for school, and then drove them there when they were in elementary school, and he did so by choice. Renée Davis still fondly recalls the breakfast her father prepared: "The food that I like for breakfast is the food that my daddy always made me for breakfast. And that's what I still like today. I like sausage made in an iron skillet that's almost so black that it just chars it to get laid in the pan it's so good." His breakfasts were considered so delicious that even Robin and Renée's friends sometimes came by to eat before school.

Just as Burruss was the kind of father who enjoyed spending mornings with his children, he was also a very hands-on father, joining the Band Mothers club at Marietta High School when Renée was in the band. His wife says it didn't bother him at all to be the only father at the Band Mothers meetings. Moreover, he was just as present in his son Robin's youth, coaching his little league team, and later attending all of Robin's basketball and football games when his son was an athlete at Marietta High School.

He would eventually become president of the Western Marietta Little League, even though, as his son points out,

> My dad, honestly, he wasn't real athletic. Growing up, I think he worked all the time and didn't play a lot so he wasn't real athletic. He wasn't the most coordinated guy. [...] [yet] he stepped up to coach when some of the nine-year-old kids were as good as he was. But he wasn't intimidated by his lack of ability or experience.

In Robin's retelling of his father's coaching, the can-do quality that Burruss later evinced in his rise in the state legislature is apparent. Usually when he set out to accomplish something, he was successful, and not simply from ambition, but from a vision he had of improving things. Robin's ball team played in Custer Park, which he says,

> was just a pasture; it wasn't anything very nice. But [Dad] had a little vision for it, and this could be more for the kids and my kids and the community. So he worked first as a coach and then his leadership, you know, always rises to the top. And so people began to look up to him for guidance and one thing led to another and they wound up sort of rebuilding the whole ballpark and he wound up being the president of Custer ballpark for like two years in a row for my eleven-year-old and twelve-year-old seasons... he showed leadership even though he didn't have the athletic ability.

That he made his family his first priority is one of the things his children remember so vividly about Burruss. Robin remembers an incident when his father regretted not spending even more time with his children, though neither he nor Renée could remember a time when he wasn't there for their practices and games. Robin recalls a conversation he had with his father where his father was encouraging him to spend more time with his children, "'I really wish that I had done more of that.' And I looked at him and I said, 'Dad, I don't remember a time ever that you weren't there for me and everything I did.' And he said something that still stays with me. He said, 'well, you may have got enough of it, but I never did.'"

Though his family was his first priority, as his wife is quick to point out, his constituents and "those that were waiting out there for him to deal with them politically" thought of themselves as his top priority. As she says, he "just had a great knack for making you feel like, I'm here for you. [...] And never having anything else on his mind or thinking that I can't deal with you today." Unlike the ubiquitous cell phones in use today, Burruss set his pager to vibrate when he was at home with his family. Still, the only time he got away from the claims of business and later, legislation, occurred when he was driving. As Renée tells it, "he used to say the only time he ever got any peace and quiet was when he got in the car."

As a state representative, Burruss certainly had his share of calls from constituents whenever he was home. His wife had a particularly harrowing experience during one such call that she took while he was out. A woman called to complain that Burruss had not been returning the calls she'd been making to his office to get his help with something she wanted. This accusation particularly upset Bobbi Burruss because she felt it was an insult to her husband, and not true besides, because he was always returning calls. In trying to impress this fact on the caller, Bobbi forgot that she had been cooking and the stove caught fire, ruining the newly remodeled kitchen. Her husband later made a joke out of this incident, and, neglecting to say the kitchen had been newly remodeled before the fire, told Celestine Sibley, "Four thousand dollars worth of damage. I sometimes accuse Bobbie [sic] of letting it happen so she could get a new kitchen."[41] Still, Burruss did help the caller, who, Bobbi says called several years later to apologize for being rude and to tell her "she had never had nobody work with her like

Al did and [she had] got whatever it was she wanted." As his wife contends, "There were people who did not return calls, but Al Burruss was never one of them, never."

Another incident she recalls illustrates one of the primary reasons Burruss enjoyed being in politics—he liked helping people. A couple called to thank him for helping get a brother in a nursing home when no one else had offered to help though they had contacted people "all the way from Washington right on down"; as he explained to Bobbi, "Now that's why I keep on keeping on. [...] That's why I stay in politics I guess."

Generous with his time, Burruss was equally generous with his money. He helped his family, setting his father up in business so that he finally knew a measure of success in later life. But Burruss helped just about anyone who approached him. The stories of his generosity are legendary among those who knew him best. Robin Burruss says he continues to hear stories of how his father took care of others, which he explains as the result of his father's own poverty growing up: "He never forgot what it was like to have nothing. So he would always help people. I still hear stories. 'Your daddy paid my utility bill one time' or those kind of things about, you know, a lot of stuff that nobody ever knew. But he sure endeared himself to a lot of people because he cared about them." At least partly, Burruss's acts of caring and charity came from his religious sensibility, for, as his son contends, "he was always motivated correctly to do the right thing because of his faith." There are tales of how he helped out single mothers who worked at the Capitol with small gifts of cash, always given anonymously, of how he always carried cash so he could give money to the homeless whenever he encountered them, of helping anyone he saw whose car had broken down on the road, of making loans, large and small, to anyone who approached him with a story of need. His wife tells one story of how he had helped out one of his Sunday school students with a small loan so she could get her car fixed and Burruss never told anyone of this help; he just quietly performed what service he could. Bobbi Burruss only found out about the loan to the student because the young woman repaid the money long after Burruss had died, sending the money to Bobbi with a note about how Burruss had helped her and she had forgotten to repay him but now that she'd remembered, she felt she must do so. There are the stories of how he provided funds to little league teams and gifts of chicken at Christmas when he was in the state legislature. Some of the people who received these gifts of chicken said that without his help, their children would not have had food to eat during the holidays. A running story that is repeated by several people who knew him is that the managers at Tip Top Poultry threatened to take away his key to the freezer because he gave away so much chicken. Yet, A. L. Burruss never asked for thanks or wanted to be acknowledged for giving. One story goes that after he died, it was discovered that he had been a significant contributor to the Calvary Children's Home in Smyrna though it had not been known during his lifetime. Even as he lay dying, he asked that people not send him flowers or gifts but rather that they make donations to the Calvary Children's Home.

Politically, Burruss was also generous, helping Jimmy Carter in all three of his campaigns, as will be discussed later in this book. The true measure of A. L. Burruss lies in his acts of love and service to his family, his friends, his employees, his constituents, and eventually, to all of the people of Georgia, whom he served throughout the fifty-eight years of his too-short life. As the next chapters will illustrate, the traits of hard work, dedication, and selfles's generosity would take him first into local political office, then into the Georgia General Assembly.

CHAPTER 2

AMBITION AND AVOCATION: BURRUSS ENTERS PUBLIC SERVICE

Whether it was in business or politics, Al Burruss was a man determined to succeed. He overcame the harsh reality of growing up in poverty. Though his father worked, he was unable to provide a steady income. Thus, Burruss worked hard and did his best to help support the family, working at any job that came his way all through his youth, including working as the school janitor in order to be able to attend high school. Rather than becoming embittered and angry by the harshness of his life and lack of financial means for a college education, Burruss was determined to make a success of his life. He took the skills the US Naval Reserve gave him in the Philippines and turned them to good use once he returned to Georgia by starting up a refrigeration business with an office on the Atlanta Highway. Later, he opened an appliance store in downtown Smyrna. But it was the refrigeration business that took him out into the community. As related in the previous chapter, he designed and built a walk-in freezer for the business owners of a small poultry processing plant in Marietta that led eventually to his purchase of the business from the two partners, E. T. Banks and Vernon Green. He so impressed Banks that he even helped finance the purchase of the plant. One of the most important attributes Burruss had was the ability to make friends and enlist others in helping him succeed.

It was no small matter for Burruss to add the running of a poultry processing plant to his growing list of business successes. And it says a lot about his character and belief in himself to move into an entirely new field, learning it from the bottom up—he plunged into learning everything, from how to "pluck chickens" to how to find suppliers, to selling his product and figuring out how to draw around him the people who could help him succeed. Of course, it was entirely natural that he would ask his best friend, Chet Austin, to join him in the new business venture; after all, they had worked together as boys and young men and knew each other's strengths and weaknesses.

The two of them forged a unique partnership with Burruss being the front man, working with customers and the community by doing the buying and selling, and Austin running the financial side of things. Austin learned how to do payroll and the accounting, doing the work, he says, of seven or eight accountants. The original plant saw them "running production lines of 2000–2500 chickens a day." In short order, they doubled that to four thousand eight hundred a day. In order to grow the business, Austin explains, "Al worked through a feed company in Cartersville. We even grew some chickens. Eventually we started doing business with folks in the county." Typically, they would call on sellers and customers in "Cartersville, Adairsville, and Calhoun in the early morning, then drive home to work in the plant."[1]

Burruss's brother Jimmie also eventually came to work for him at Tip Top. In 1970 his brother Buddy joined the firm; Buddy had worked for his father in a successful wholesale egg business until the father sold it. Though Tip Top Poultry had only twenty-five employees when Burruss took over in 1951, within two decades, it had grown to four hundred employees processing six thousand chickens an hour, with plants in Marietta and Holly Springs and nationwide business connections.[2]

The original processing plant is described by Chet Austin as a "little hole in the wall—radiator shop on one side and mule barn on the other side," almost in downtown Marietta.[3] When the Urban Renewal Program of the 1950s came into Marietta, Austin said he and Al realized their business was "a prospect and they were going to buy us out and we were going to have to move." Though he and Al began to scout for a new location, Austin points out that "Al did most of this. We walked every sewer line in Cobb County—not many at that time. We had to have a sewage line because we generate a lot of sewage. We settled on a site on Sandtown Road." Unfortunately, when they applied for zoning, the owner across the street from the site opposed the application. Austin remembers that at the zoning hearing, the property owner had all his neighbors there to oppose the plan as well, so Burruss and Austin withdrew their proposal. Their next move was a catastrophe that ended well, as Austin recalls:

> This time we made a big mistake, bought a piece of property on what's now part of Southern Poly, just off the four lane, already zoned. We cleared the property, designed the building and ordered the steel. A friend of ours had cleared it and piled up debris and set it afire. All that potash floated up and into a motel swimming pool [owned by] Lance Murray, an old Tech football player. He was going to enjoin us and get rid of us. This time we went to Herbert McCollum, the sole county commissioner and told him we were going to have to leave the county. He said he had 10 acres on Wallace Road (actually the county's property). Five acres were promised for a school but he agreed to sell the other five to us, at $1000 an acre. Over the years, we accumulated about 20 more acres.[4]

Because they had already purchased the steel, they moved it to the new location, and Tip Top Poultry's headquarters is still located today at the Wallace Road facility.

Burruss's numerous business commitments draw a portrait of a man who did not sit still for long. During the 1950s and 1960s, Burruss worked on growing his businesses. In addition to the poultry processing business, he and Austin also acquired an interest in a feed mill in Cedartown.[5] At one point, while serving as President of Tip Top Poultry, which he would do until his death in 1986, Burruss also managed other firms and sat on their boards of directors: Marietta Poultry Equipment, Inc.; Poultry Specialties, Inc.; Cobb Poultry Transport, Inc.; Kennesaw Mountain Poultry Inc.; Cedar Valley Mills, Inc., where he served as chairman of the board; Cedar Valley Poultry, Inc.; and Cedartown Dairy Products, Inc.[6] He and a brother-in-law, Gordon Haines, also jointly owned a car dealership in Cornelia for a time. As if his business responsibilities were not sufficient to keep him fully engaged, he also served as director of the Georgia Poultry Federation and as director and vice president of the Georgia Poultry Processors Association.[7] In 1962, Burruss was named the Area Young Man of the Year by the Jaycees for his active leadership in many areas, from "church and little league baseball activities" to his directorships.[8]

No one recalls, from his family to his friends and business associates, A. L. ever shirking any of his many duties, whether they be familial or corporate. Even his wife Bobbi Burruss expresses surprise at all her husband managed to do: "There was just no way he could have done everything he did and never let one go. I don't care if it was a problem or if it was just something good. He had time to deal with it and did. I don't know where it came from and I lived with the man."[9] In a brief interchange during an interview, Bobbi and her daughter Renée relate how Burruss seemed to have an abundance of time for everything:

> **Bobbi:** He just had a great knack for making you feel like I'm here for you.
>
> **Renée:** And that there was nothing else more important than doing that right.
>
> **Bobbi:** And never having anything else on his mind or something that I can't deal with you today. There again came that time element. We don't know where he got it. It was a gift.

If Burruss worked hard, he also took time to play, too. Introduced to flying in his late teens by his friend Art Godwin, it became an enjoyable part of his life and later played an important role in Jimmy Carter's two campaigns for governor of Georgia. As mentioned previously, in the late 1940s he courted Bobbi on his weekends off from work by flying up to Cornelia to be with her. Eventually, he earned an instrument-rated pilot's license and acquired more sophisticated planes. When his son Robin was in his teens, Burruss flew him and his friends to the Bahamas for scuba diving excursions. The family also acquired a houseboat on Lake Allatoona and spent many summers there. Despite his obvious successes and great self-discipline evident elsewhere in his life, the one thing Burruss couldn't lick was his lifelong smoking habit. At one point, Burruss decided he wanted to quit smoking (he was, by various accounts, either a two- or four-packs-a-day smoker).[10] In order to do this, he holed up in the houseboat for a week with no cigarettes. Food was brought out to him by his family. But at the end of the week, Burruss acknowledged he just could not quit smoking, so gave up the effort.[11]

Becoming a successful businessman enabled Burruss to achieve a comfortable lifestyle that far surpassed the lowly expectations of his youth; but being a businessman was just not enough to satisfy him.

As his business acumen grew, he began to look for other opportunities to engage his active mind and restless ambition. By the mid-1960s, the governance structure of Cobb County changed from a single-member county commission to a five-member county commission and thus created an opportunity for successful businessmen, like Burruss, to enter politics. As Thomas Scott, whose history of Cobb County thoroughly covers every aspect of the county's growth and its people during the twentieth century, tells it, times were ripe for change: "The year 1964 was a turning point in Cobb County.... With over 130,000 people, Cobb County was ready for a more representative form of government that could balance the needs of newcomers and old-timers, suburbanites, city dwellers, and a dwindling number of rural residents."[12] Initially, the Cobb delegation representatives to the General Assembly were divided over how to set up the county commission. Joe Mack Wilson wanted a five-man commission with an appointed county manager.[13] However, the referendum that Cobb County voters eventually rejected in January 1964 was a compromise suggested by Bob Flournoy for a "three-member commission without a county manager."[14] The final bill that went to Cobb voters, who approved it in July 1964, was one Bob Flournoy drew up. Flournoy's bill was modeled on the DeKalb County system, as Scott notes, of "four part-time district commissioners and a full-time chairman who would serve as chief executive officer.... Terms of office were set at four years with one eastern and one western commissioner initially elected for two years to provide staggered terms."[15] As one of Cobb County's most successful businessmen, Burruss believed he had a lot to offer in the form of solid experience and he had ambitions to become more involved in local government.

Once the five-member county commission was approved, he threw his hat into the ring for the four-year term for the western district (Post 4). Though his campaign was low-key, he ran ads in *The Marietta Daily Journal* that cited his business experience as his key qualification for a position on the commission. His large, extended family became his most ardent supporters as his campaign staff. The primary ad run by his campaign in *The Marietta Daily Journal*, beginning in August 1964 and running up to the election on November 3, 1964, introduced voters to the young businessman. This ad began by citing his accomplishments, leading off with his personal statistics, "age 37, married and father of two children," then moved on to his experience, which showcased his background as a businessman, family man, and church leader:

> Businessman in Cobb County for 15 years; President-General manager of Tip Top Poultry—a leading Cobb County industry; Past President Georgia Poultry Processors Association; Director of National Broiler Council; Member Board of Stewards, Tillman Memorial Methodist Church—Smyrna; Marietta's Young Man of the Year, 1962; Past President Marietta Western Little League.

The ad's focus, "Al Makes One Promise," emphasized his business acumen and faith, which he was putting at the disposal of Cobb County voters: "To use my extensive business experience and other God Given abilities to administer the affairs of Cobb County in an honorable and efficient manner."[16] The ad also included a picture of the attractive young man.

Another campaign ad that ran in September of 1964 describes a style of campaigning that Al employed again when he ran for state representative and later for Speaker pro tempore of the House—visiting as many of the constituents as could be seen in the time allowed in order to persuade them that he was the right man for the job. This campaign ad had far more narrative than his other ads, which may explain why it only ran once.

> During the few brief weeks of this campaign it has been my pleasure to visit with old friends, renew acquaintances and to make many new friends among the voters of Cobb

County. I earnestly regret that the limited time for the campaign precludes my visiting with each voter in the County's Western District to discuss affairs that are vital to the progress of our County.

What is clear from this ad is how Burruss positions himself as an "honest and impartial" representative on whom the voters can depend, one who fills the need for "experienced, qualified and dedicated men for positions of leadership."[17] His self-described dedication assures voters not only of his competence but also of his will to do good service: "I am vitally interested in Cobb County and I believe my 15 years business experience here provides me with a background that will be beneficial in solving the problems that face us. I assure you that I can and will cooperate with all other County officials in any endeavor that is in the best interest of and for the benefit of Cobb County." Again, the long narrative of the ad ends with his "one promise," a statement that appears in all the ads he ran for county commissioner.

Two other ads also appeared in the Marietta paper, each emphasizing his "one promise."[18] The second of these small ads—the "Burruss Not Elected!" ad—has a seemingly humorous and catchy opening line, meant to get voters to the poll if they wanted him elected. Yet, the real purpose for such a warning stemmed from the fact that the Republican Party had held its first local primary and was making its first serious races in Cobb that year (Goldwater became the first Republican to carry the county in a presidential election, and Republican Ben Jordan knocked Bob Flournoy out of his county-wide seat in the legislature). Burruss wanted to make sure that Democrats didn't forget to go to the polls. Since the Democratic primary had decided everything in past elections, there would be a tendency for the voters to think that the election was over after the primary.[19]

As in earlier campaign ads, this one points out the key attributes Burruss always cited in his political campaigns, and in all his affairs: that his abilities came from God, his management skills would be put to good use for the people, he is a man of his word, and his integrity and business skills would ensure he would serve the people well.

In the final count of the votes, Ernest Barrett won the run-off to become commission chair, and in the other positions were Bill Oliver, Harry

Ingram, Tommy Brown, and Al Burruss.[20] Although Burruss, running as a Democrat, faced opposition from Republican F. Y. Dillingham, he won the election for a four-year term beginning January 2, 1965. *The Marietta Daily Journal* posted his winning tally: "Burruss was winner in Acworth 639 to 558, Big Shanty [Kennesaw] 557 to 349, Fair Oaks 1,940 to 1,364, Lost Mountain 94 to 50, Oregon 166 to 145, Powder Springs 561 to 421, Red Rock 96 to 42, Ward Two 961 to 307, Ward Three 696 to 160, Ward Four 288 to 106 and Ward Eight 229 to 138."[21] Overall, "Burruss scored a 58 percent victory over Dillingham."[22]

Once the new five-member Cobb County Commission began its bimonthly meetings, Burruss quickly established that he had his own ideas about how an efficient government should be run. At the first meeting, on January 12, 1965, he and Tommy Brown opposed the plan proposed by Harry Ingram to retain a law firm to handle the county's legal issues; instead, they thought hiring a lawyer at a salary of $15,000 would be preferable to the open-ended billing of a legal firm. They argued that the county had spent $25,000 the previous year with such a system. But Ingram's proposal was approved, three to two, with Burruss and Brown voting against the plan.[23] As Thomas Scott points out in his history of Cobb County, "From the beginning the county commission split its votes on policy questions with Chairman Barrett and eastern district commissioner Bill Oliver (or his replacement, T. L. Dickson) on one side, western district commissioner Al Burruss and Tommy Brown on the other, and eastern district commissioner Harry Ingram the swing vote."[24] Burruss, a fiscal conservative like most Georgia Democrats of the 1960s, was always looking for ways to save money, and he was not afraid to push his own agenda once he became part of the decision-making process.

Toward the end of his tenure on the commission, he showed great satisfaction from the accomplishments of the airport committee, of which he was chair: "'I'm as proud of what we've done at the airport as anything else we've done,' he said, citing the additional hangar space, the second fixed base operation now located there and the fact that twice as many airplanes are based there now."[25] Yet, he appeared generally pleased with the commission's work in general, claiming, "I'm extremely proud of what we've done. I think Cobb County has a new face and I think we're partially responsible for it."[26] However, serving on the Cobb County Commission did not provide Burruss with the reach he desired and midway during his term as a commissioner, Burruss decided to run for a higher political office in the state government. In 1968, he announced he would not be seeking a second term on the commission but instead would be running for a legislative seat in the General Assembly. The legislative seats in the House of Representatives had been reapportioned so that in the November election of 1968, Cobb and Paulding counties were combined into one large district with seven representatives running at-large.[27] This change presented Burruss with an ideal opportunity to parlay his experience in county government into a larger forum. Chet Austin doesn't recall a particular moment when Burruss chose to run for higher office, just that he made up his mind he wanted to go to the state House.[28] No one in his family remembers the day he decided to run either; but regardless of the reason, his decision was in keeping with his desire to serve others. It may have been his meeting of Jimmy Carter, the state senator from Plains, Georgia, that encouraged him to run for higher office.

Once Al Burruss met Jimmy Carter the two forged a friendship that would see them through Carter's presidency right up to Burruss's death in 1986. In a television program about Burruss produced in 1992, Carter recalled how their friendship developed:

> When I began my campaign for governor, I was kind of a lonely candidate without many friends in the state, not very much money, not any way to get around and seek votes except to drive my own car. Then I met Al Burruss who volunteered to help me with the campaign. He had an airplane then, which was a wonderful phenomenon in my life, and he was very generous in helping me to get to know Georgia. It was a very large contribution personally, but the main advantage I derived from it was not just to get from one place to another in the state, but to spend those hours of travel forming a relationship with Al Burruss that was precious to me.[29]

Though Carter lost his first gubernatorial race, "finishing third to former governor Ellis Arnall and flamboyant restaurateur Lester Maddox,"[30] Burruss continued to believe in Carter's ability to win and govern well the state of Georgia. Burruss supported Carter again in his second gubernatorial run in 1970, the implications of which will be discussed further in the next chapter.

Before Burruss determined to run for state representative, however, he first contemplated running for the seat of state Senator Sam Hensley, who was thinking of running for the congressional seat of Representative John W. Davis.[31] Though he expressed a definite interest in running for the Senate, Burruss himself appeared undecided about staying in politics, saying he had not yet "made up his mind whether to 'run for commissioner, run for the senate or go home."[32] *The Marietta Daily Journal* reported that he had considered resigning from the commission in early 1967 for business reasons, but changed his mind. In any event, Hensley resolved to seek reelection to the state senate, so Burruss let pass the idea of running for the Senate though not the idea of running for state office.

When Burruss announced in April 1968 that he would not seek a second term on the county commission, it became obvious that he had begun to think seriously of running for state representative. The primary reason for giving up his seat on the commission, as he told *The Marietta Daily Journal* involved his business obligations. He was "developing a new business corporation in addition to several of which he already is an officer."[33] Though others had been aware that he had been reconsidering his position on the commission for some time, he now claimed that his three years on the commission had "been a frustrating time."[34] While it could be assumed that the frustration he expressed might have something to do with being too often on the losing side of the decisions being made by the commission, he found it more difficult to split his time between his businesses and the commission. His announcement included the statement that his time might be better spent in the House of Representatives than the commission because, he says, "I can take two months away from the business better than I can take half of every day and half of every night."[35] Such a conception of time could have only been a subterfuge to dodge the question of whether or not he would run for state representative, for Burruss was too smart a man not to be aware that the work of a state representative goes on all year long, not just in the two-month General Assembly session. At any rate, he soon declared his candidacy for state representative.

Naturally, Burruss recruited all his family and friends to help him campaign for the state legislature. Austin tells an anecdote about a campaign handout that illustrates Burruss's type of involvement: "[The] first novelty item was a fly swatter—ordered about 10,000. We handed them out on Saturday morning at service stations and restaurants; we worked hard but got rid of them. Next Tuesday, we came in and there was that many more of them. Al had come in, seen they were all gone and ordered another batch. We realized he was going to do his own thing."[36]

Just as his earlier ad for commissioner had cited his business experience in support of his candidacy, so too did his ad for state representative, except he now had his experience as a commissioner to add to his credibility. Interestingly, the 1968 campaign ad appears to use the same photograph used in his 1964 campaign. This race would be much tougher than his campaign for county commissioner, for he was attempting to unseat incumbent Homer Leggett of Paulding County.

Shortly before the primary elections, the Women Voter's organization put together a questionnaire asking all the candidates in the House and Senate races about issues important to Cobb voters, then printed the candidates' answers in *The Marietta Daily Journal* on September 8, 1968. In response to the question, "What particular qualifications do you have which you feel would make you the best person for this office?" Burruss cited his very extensive business experience, listing nine firms in which he had 20 years of managerial experience, then listing his term as a Cobb County commissioner.[37] For most of the questions, his responses were brief and to the point, usually one sentence and not very provocative. For example, when asked "What is your interpretation of the 'Home Rule for Counties' law as passed by the Georgia State Legislature in 1966, and how can this law be best applied to the problems facing Cobb County?" Burruss gave the careful response, "This bill must be ratified by the voters and probably tested in the courts. If approved many Cobb County problems can be controlled by this law."[38] It was the sort of answer that Burruss often provided about an issue when he wanted time to mull the issue over, thus avoiding committing himself before having done so. It is also the sort of answer that one would expect from an experienced businessman, one not given to sudden decisions without forethought, and such studied answers would be

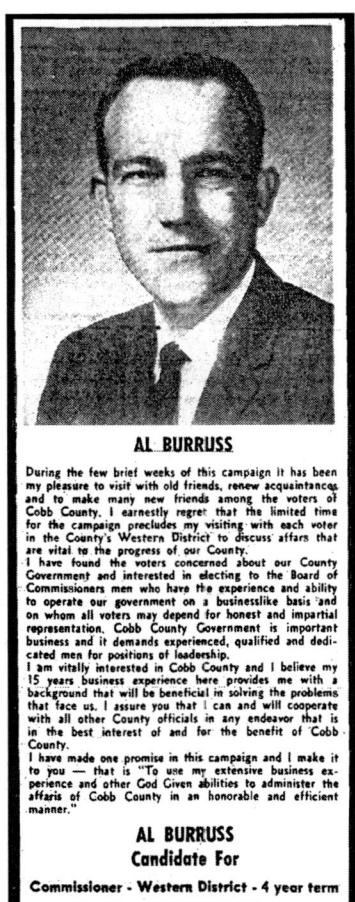

(Left) The most frequent campaign advertisement that appeared weekly in the newspaper during August–November of 1964. (Right) Another advertisement that appeared on September 8, 1964.

ideal for a state representative. He provided a similar answer to the question, "In your opinion what would be specific advantages and/or disadvantages to including Cobb County in Rapid Transit?" He said, "[MARTA] must tell us what facilities will be provided for Cobb County and also what the true cost will be, then their proposal can be evaluated." As a fiscal conservative, Burruss was not about to commit the people of Cobb County to increased taxation unless it was beneficial to them, and this issue had already sparked huge controversy in Cobb County, where voters were gearing up to fight joining the Metropolitan Atlanta Rapid Transit Authority (MARTA). In a referendum to approve joining the MARTA, Cobb County had voted the act down in 1965, and its future in Cobb County was unsure at best when Burruss was running for representative.[39]

Burruss's humanism can be seen in his response to the question, "Do you favor an increase in the amount of state revenue used to aid urban problems?" because he showed a preference for those whom he thought were truly helpless, which interestingly did not include those on welfare. He answered, "Yes, in mental health and other areas where people are not able to help themselves, not in giveaway programs that encourage people to loaf." But his approach to taxing the people also shows he cared for those with special needs. To the question, "If there is a need for increased State revenue, how would you propose raising it?" he presented sound advice: "(1) By closing loop-holes in our tax laws that allow some people and business [sic] to escape paying their fair share. (2) By promoting new industry and business that will increase revenue without increasing the demand for other services. (3) By raising sales tax rate and allocating the proceeds to special needs." The plan he outlined would be one he followed during his long tenure in the House. Raising the sales tax became a favored way for the legislature to pay for services.

Though running against a Democratic incumbent, Burruss had proven himself as a commissioner and *The Marietta Daily Journal* endorsed him for the House seat. Editor Dick West, referring to Burruss as a "guiding force" behind the renewed political life in Cobb County thanks to the work of the new commission, praised him for bringing his successful business practices to bear in his service on the commission: "he has been a leader in guiding the administration of Cobb County onto a more forward-looking, more representative track during the past four years," and "has established himself as a sound thinker, a man of principle and an able exponent of progress."[40] Moreover, the endorsement claimed Burruss had "earned the privilege of representing Cobb and Paulding counties in the legislature."[41]

Whether or not the people of Cobb and Paulding counties agreed with West that Burruss had "earned" his entry into the legislature was not readily apparent. Though neither Leggett nor Burruss appeared to have any doubts about the outcome, Burruss only narrowly defeated Leggett by 143 votes in the September 11, 1968, Democratic primary election.[42] In the initial tally, "Burruss received 12,910 votes in Cobb and 980 votes in Paulding for a total of 13,890. Leggett polled 9,453 here and 4,169 in his home county for a total vote of 13,712."[43] Leggett immediately contested the results through his attorney, who claimed that " 'several hundred' votes incorrectly voided by poll officials would make his client the winner."[44] There were some voting discrepancies that seem reminiscent of the twentieth century's problems with "chads" in the Florida election of George W. Bush. A new ballot was being used that called for voters to mark the ballots to indicate the candidate they were voting for, but numerous voters in Paulding County "improperly marked" their ballots and consequently, these were thrown out. A further complication was reported on the Op-Ed page of *The Marietta Daily Journal*: "questions also have been raised as to why the Paulding County vote count was not completed until midway through the day following the election, and why it was still another day later before the county chairman would certify the Paulding returns."[45] Though Leggett initially called for a recount of the votes, the recount of Hiram Precinct ballots only netted him another 35 votes; Leggett went away for the weekend to mull things over, then decided to concede the race to Burruss.[46] In all probability, he conceded rather than fought for a recount because he had hoped to fill the suddenly vacant Senate seat resulting from the death of Senator Albert Moore," but did not get elected to the seat by the four-county Democratic committee.[47]

In the general election that November, Al Burruss was elected, along with all other Democratic candidates for the House and Senate.[48] An ad that ran in *The Marietta Daily Journal* in early November made voting for Cobb Democrats easy to do, telling voters that "By punching hole no. 22 you will be voting the straight State and Local Democratic ticket."[49] It was an interesting election though not that unusual for Cobb County, for Nixon was elected president and carried the county, yet all six Republican legislative candidates were defeated. This split was typical, of course, for Georgia and many other southern states at that time—to vote Republican for president and Democratic for other office seekers. Besides Burruss, there were three other first-time legislators, George Kreeger Jr., Howard Atherton, and

Eugene Housley.⁵⁰ Rounding out the nine-member all-Democratic Cobb delegation in the 1969 session were incumbent representatives Joe Mack Wilson, Hugh Lee McDaniell, and Cyrus M. Chapman, and Senators J. H. Henderson and Sam P. Hensley.⁵¹ With this election win, Burruss began the first of nine consecutive terms as a state legislator, remaining in office until his death.

Burruss primed himself to be an assertive, informed legislator. As he did whenever he was faced with learning something new, he made a careful and thoughtful study of each issue that came before him before giving his own opinions. Shortly after the election, he began a study of the Georgia Tax Revision Study Commission report and expressed his opinion freely to the reporters who began approaching him. His disgust with the report is obvious: "the inaction 'came as a real blow to me. I was depending on them to show me the way. It looks like they wasted a lot of time and a lot of money.'"⁵² One thing he did not care for, especially as a successful businessman, was a waste of time and taxpayers' money and this was something he felt he could change. Another part of his learning approach was done by attending meetings aimed at educating new legislators. At one such meeting in Athens, held in December of 1968, he was upset to learn that state funds set aside for maintaining juvenile homes across the state appeared not to have been allocated fairly in Cobb County and announced plans to do something about it: "Burruss feels the county is getting short-changed to an extent and told Shipley last week he intends to introduce some kind of legislation that will remedy the situation."⁵³ We see him here, a new legislator, not even sworn in yet, but ready to do battle for the things he believes in. He studied how to be a legislator and talked to everyone he could to learn how to be effective, but when he did not know enough, he was unafraid to say so:

> Rep.-elect Al Burruss said he understood from talking to highway officials that more money was needed for maintenance, but added that he had not had time to study the pro[p]osal being made by the department.⁵⁴ One can see his eagerness to get started when asked his opinion of what the 1969 General Assembly's business will be, replying that

he was "looking forward to learning the mechanics of the General Assembly, [that] poor legislation is worse than none at all."[55]

Moreover, his feistiness and his willingness to do what was necessary to get the job done was evident in how he thought the new budget would get approved. As *The Marietta Daily Journal* reported, "He said he thought there would be a 'lot of head-knocking' over taxes and the budget which would end in compromise."[56]

Just as he had done when he first became a commissioner, he developed his own agenda, often based on what he was hearing from his constituents, and presented it. For example, he introduced a resolution addressed to the US Congress to change the ending of daylight savings time in Georgia at "midnight Labor Day instead of the last Sunday of October" because he said "he had heard more complaints about Daylight Savings Time than any other problems, including taxes."[57] Nor was he worried about reversing himself, even when his opinions had been expressed in the newspaper. Having told *The Marietta Daily Journal* reporter Bill Schemmel that "he would vote for increases on wine and cigarette tax,"[58] he shortly thereafter voted against the tax increase on cigarettes.[59] When the House Urban Caucus organized by Joe Mack Wilson and Howard Atherton proposed a local option sales tax, Burruss showed his independent thinking by saying "he was not certain that the state needs the proposed increase in corporate and individual tax."[60] As his first session as a legislator ended in March 1969, Burruss had begun the learning process that would make him one of the most respected legislators in the General Assembly. The next chapter will illustrate his growing confidence and competence as he learned how to the things he wanted to accomplish.

CHAPTER 3

STATE REPRESENTATIVE A. L. BURRUSS: THE EARLY YEARS, 1970–1976

In 1992, six years after Burruss's death from pancreatic cancer, Georgia Public Television and Kennesaw State University (then Kennesaw State College) made a film in honor of A. L. Burruss about his career in the Georgia General Assembly. This film highlights two aspects of Burruss's career in the 1970s that had a major impact on him personally. One was his friendship and support of Jimmy Carter through two gubernatorial races and his run for president. The other was Burruss's own ambitions, his method of gaining support, and how he recovered from his first major failure as a state representative. These two things say much about Burruss's development as a politician and how his success grew in the 1970s and 1980s from that of a novice to a powerful force to be reckoned with in the House.

Though Carter had lost his first bid for governor of Georgia in 1966, he ran again in 1970. Burruss, who once more loaned Carter his plane to travel around Georgia, often served as pilot for these trips. Paul Shields, former anchor at WAGA-TV in Atlanta, narrated the film about Burruss's political life and had this to say about the friendship that developed between Carter and Burruss: "When Carter was campaigning for governor, Al Burruss's plane and pilot's license became indispensable to the campaign. While they were crisscrossing the state, they got to know each other very well; they became friends. After Carter was elected, he made Al his floor leader in the Georgia House of Representatives."[1] The trust Carter placed in Burruss was based on their friendship and mutual respect although, as Shields pointed out, it also presented Burruss with a tremendous burden: "Floor leader for Governor Carter. This was quite a beginning for a new legislator. Burruss was hard-pressed. Time now must be spent between Cobb's needs, his poultry business, and keeping Governor Carter's proposals intact."[2]

Burruss's role in Governor Carter's new programs was not an easy one; as Carter himself described it:

> We tried to reorganize the entire state of Georgia's government. It hadn't been done since 1932 when Senator Russell had been the governor of Georgia. And we tangled with a lot of powerful special interest groups, some of them quite benevolent in character but they had carved out for themselves hundreds of little agencies and bureaus and so forth, turf that was precious to them and there was a tremendous waste of Georgia's money and it was very complicated administrating the affairs of a great state but Al Burruss as my floor leader was able to husband these extremely controversial and important legislative proposals through the House of Representatives. Quite often they were not friendly to what we proposed.[3]

Gary M. Fink, in *Prelude to the Presidency*, describes the ambitious agenda Carter laid out even before he took office as governor, a plan that included not only reorganization of state government, but also included initiating "programs in such politically volatile areas as welfare reform, tax policy, conservation, education, judicial reform, and consumer protection."[4] Carter was successful in getting the reorganization plan carried out, as well as most of the programs he laid out, except for his consumer protection plan.[5] Moreover, Carter did not govern in the manner of traditional Georgia politicians; he refused to grant favors in exchange for votes. As Carter's floor leader, Al Burruss was charged with getting the House legislators on board so legislation could be passed.

Burruss was obviously a good choice for such a role, even if he was fairly new to the legislature. Senator Steve Thompson of Cobb County, who served alongside Burruss in the House before election to the Senate, explains Burruss's powers of persuasion: "Al was a trader. He was able to work with people of all echelons.... he could talk to people with limited educations or he could hold PhD's in the palm of his hand."[6] Terry Lawler, also a fellow state legislator and a friend of Burruss's, says that "Al could bring people together, even when they were in severe and acrimonious conflict with each other."[7] Looking back at his association with Burruss, Jimmy Carter recalls the traits that made Al special: "So what Al brought was a remarkable combination of basic personal integrity—he was honest in every way; he told the truth, he didn't exaggerate, he was very modest.... Al was never reluctant to say this was a bad idea, you've made a mistake here; I think you should do something different. And that's where the value comes in of dealing with someone with that degree of strength and personal friendship and integrity."[8]

As can be seen from Carter's memorandum to the Legislative Control Team that lays out his schedule of daily meetings, Burruss, as his floor leader in the House, had a busy workload. In addition to his work as a legislator, he was tasked by Carter, along with Al Holloway, Hugh Carter, and Frank Sutton, with bringing "together all legislators who will be involved in the key issues during the day so I can explain my position and let the legislators explain how they plan to approach the problem and what action the other legislators and I need to take."[9] In the first session of Carter's term as governor, Burruss helped House Bill No. 1 get through the House; this bill ensured that the reorganization plan for state government "would automatically become law after the beginning of the next legislative session, unless vetoed by a majority in the house and the senate"; it only passed by one vote, but it gave Carter the mandate he needed to move forward.[10] Burruss had his work cut out for him during Carter's term, for the governor had few friends in the legislature. Fink reports an incident when a reporter asked Burruss to identify Carter's supporters in the House and Al quipped, "It's not going to be a long article, is it?"[11] Serving as Carter's floor leader, however, also had its perks, one being that Burruss gained increasing recognition, a factor that aided him in his legislative ambitions.

When House Speaker George L. Smith, II died early in December of 1973, it was expected that Speaker pro tempore Tom Murphy would move into the Speaker position, which would then leave his position open.[12] George Busbee briefly considered running for Speaker but decided not to as he was considering a run for governor in 1974.[13] With Tom Murphy stepping into the Speaker's slot, this left the Speaker pro tempore position open and Burruss quickly announced he would be a candidate.[14] Opposing him was Representative Bill Lee, among others. Frederick Burger, writing in *The Marietta Daily Journal*, pointed out that Burruss's drawbacks for the position were his short time in office—Lee had served in the House since 1957 while Burruss first achieved office in 1969—and Burruss's close affiliation with Carter, who was unpopular in the House.[15] In an interesting comment, however, Burger noted that Burruss had split with Carter in the previous year because Burruss had failed to become director of the new Department of Transportation, which was created in the reorganization.[16] This "split" is difficult to credit since Burruss remained friends with Carter and later supported him in his run for the presidency. Moreover, Burruss was still, at this time, Carter's administrative floor leader in the House and Burruss even mentions his work for Carter when explaining why he's the right choice to be Speaker pro tempore: "I think I have been able to keep down a lot of the controversy in the House by tempering proposals from [Governor Carter's] department heads before they reached the floor."[17]

In an unusual move, Burruss decided to take his case straight to each legislator in the House before the General Assembly reconvened in January 1975 to elect a new Speaker pro tempore. As Celestine Sibley reported, Burruss "wanted a political post [Speaker pro tempore of the Georgia House] which nobody from a metropolitan area has held in a long time. He needed the country and small towns to get it—and he went and asked them for it."[18] He got in his car the day after Christmas in 1973 and drove all over the state, visiting as many of the one hundred eighty members of the House as he could find at home, and telephoning the rest or catching them at the Capitol; he succeeded in reaching all but three of the legislators.[19] He told Sibley about his campaigning: "'Of course, they didn't all say they'd vote for me,' said the dark-haired, dark-eyed mountain-born Burruss, grinning. 'Some of them were committed to one of the other four candidates.... But it was important to talk to them and to ask them if there was a run-off if they'd support me.' "[20] There was a run-off between Burruss and Representative Williams, but Burruss won on the second ballot with eighty-four votes to Williams's sixty.[21]

Burruss was ecstatic and even cried upon attaining the desired post, saying "I'm 46 years old and I'm glad I can still cry when I'm happy."[22] Milo Dakin claimed that Burruss got a lot of supporters because he had assured Tom Murphy that he wasn't ambitious for the Speaker's post in 1975.[23] When the legislative session opened and Burruss was confirmed, he told those gathered:

> I am not a slave to any one section of the state. I am aware there are forces in state government that would like to see a feud develop in this House, but that will not happen, and Al Burruss is not looking for a fight I want you to know you have not misplaced the trust you placed in this rural chicken plucker from urban Cobb County.[24]

His address to the House members and the press illustrates a lot about Al Burruss, especially his astute political sense of how things worked in the Georgia Assembly and how to stay above the fray, even when pushing the political agenda of an unpopular governor. His speech pulls together the disparate parts of his appeal—his humble beginnings and his current urban status. This "chicken plucker" knew how to politick, and as his wife Bobbi says, he never forgot where he came from. Yet, in light of his later pursuit of the Speaker post, it may be that he was also thinking of the powerful Tom Murphy as the one with whom he might feud.

Besides getting Governor Carter's legislation introduced and passed during the early 1970s, Burruss helped "to repeal the old blue law which prohibited businesses from operating on Sunday. The law that Burruss helped pass and that Carter signed liberalized the old system by identifying 35 types of businesses that could operate on Sundays."[25] Burruss also worked for a women's credit bill that outlawed discrimination against women who wanted to borrow money.[26] While the credit bill may seem odd today, when women have the same credit rights as men, in 1974 this was very significant to the lives of women in Georgia. Another piece of legislation that Burruss supported was the Equal Rights Amendment though it failed to get ratified by the Georgia General Assembly.[27]

Terry Lawler describes Burruss's habit of playing things close to his chest: "For example, when the Cobb delegation would go to meetings (sort of town halls) on specific legislation to answer questions, discuss issues, Al kept his full opinion to himself. Where others might say they were going to vote yea or nay, Al wouldn't say. Few knew where he stood until he cast his vote publicly. So he surprised his constituents when he voted for the Equal Rights Amendment, the only legislator in the House to do so."[28] Understanding why he voted for the ratification when he had to know that his constituents in conservative Cobb and Paulding counties would not support it indicates that Burruss voted from his conscience and that he personally favored equal rights for women. Only a man supremely easy in his own skin, one who had no problem with joining the Band Mothers organization at the high school his daughter attended, would have no problems with ensuring women had equal rights under the law.

Another piece of legislation that surprised some constituents was Burruss's support of the antismoking legislation given his own heavy habit, variously reported as two or four packs of cigarettes a day. The antismoking bill made it a misdemeanor, punishable by fines, for anyone to smoke in any public area where No Smoking signs were posted.[29] Burruss told Celestine Sibley, with whom he was close friends, that he was "probably the heaviest smoker in this House—tobacco farms don't have to worry about going out of business as long as I'm alive.... I'm in serious support of this bill because I know people who are severely allergic to tobacco smoke. People ought to be able to ride elevators and public conveyances without encountering something so severely endangering."[30] From the things he said and the legislation he supported emerges a portrait of a conscientious man, one who genuinely cared about others, including the environment they lived in. Burruss cosponsored the Metropolitan Rivers Protection Act of 1974, which established "a 2,000-foot protection corridor along the Chattahoochee River and its impoundments for 48 miles between Buford Dam and Peachtree Creek."[31] He also aided the passage of the House of the Environmental Education Act of 1974, which created educational programs to further protection of the state's natural environment.[32] For his sponsorship of these two bills, Burruss was named the Georgia Legislative Conservationist of the year by the Georgia Wildlife Federation.[33]

In addition to his legislative work and running his businesses, Burruss also became George Busbee's campaign manager after the primary election in 1974. Burruss's sister Jane Ragan, who worked as a volunteer on the Busbee campaign, relates an interesting anecdote from that time. Her brother told her not to tell people she was his sister until the day after the election so no one would know she and Al were siblings. He was a father figure to her and very protective of her. She recalls that even though no one, except Busbee, knew they were related, in all that time, she "never heard one bad word about Al."[34]

Cobb historian Tom Scott tells the story of how George Busbee sought out Representatives Joe Mack Wilson and Al Burruss, Senator Roy Barnes, Harold Willingham and others to garner support in the area north of Atlanta, where Busbee had little name recognition:

> When he asked what he could do to gain their support, the Cobb countians asked for three things: the conversion of Kennesaw Junior College to senior-college status; the completion of Marietta loop, including an underpass at Atlanta Street under the railroad track; and the construction of the last leg of I-75.[35]

Scott reports that Busbee agreed with their wishes and saw to it they got what they wanted over the next four years of his term as governor.

Getting Kennesaw Junior College (KJC) elevated to senior-college status was not easy because the Board of Regents opposed such a move, as its vision of KJC, and all other junior colleges, was as a feeder school for Georgia State University.[36] Also, Chancellor George Simpson "argued that the creation of a four-year school in predominantly white Cobb County would delay the university system's efforts to meet a federal desegregation order."[37] To counter these arguments, several delegations went to the Board of Regents to argue their case, but little was done until Joe Mack Wilson, Al Burruss, and Appropriations Committee chair Joe Frank Harris managed to get $100,000 in 1975 and another $250,000 in 1976 earmarked in the state budget for converting KJC into senior-college status.[38] Another factor that Scott points out was Busbee's appointment of several new regents to the board who voted more favorably with regard to KJC's conversion.[39] Rick Beene noted that Burruss, who served on the KJC Board of Trustees, was "pivotal in getting funds for the college to become a four-year institution."[40] In an article about

Burruss, entitled "Al Burruss—Cobb's Legislative Ace," the first thing listed is the $250,000 put into the budget for converting KJC to four-year status.[41] Burruss's relationship with Governor Busbee was the second thing on the list—he was referred to as "Cobb County's ear," in the governor's office.[42]

Burruss not only supported KJC, he was also instrumental in getting Southern Tech students greater autonomy from Georgia Tech. He introduced a bill in 1975 to make Southern Tech students eligible to take the Georgia professional engineer exam one year earlier than the mandated six-year wait.[43] Though he did not succeed in always getting his agenda through the House—for example, he and Tom Murphy opposed the Sunshine Law requiring all meetings of the House be public[44]—he succeeded often enough to become a powerful force in the legislature even though he had only been there since 1969.

When Jimmy Carter ran for president in 1976, Burruss supported him though not to the extent he had been able to when Carter only needed flying around the state. Burruss had an absolute faith in Carter's ability to achieve his dream of becoming president. Former Governor Roy Barnes, who knew Burruss all his life, tells an interesting story about Burruss's belief in Carter: "I remember Al Burruss was the only person I ever met who was convinced from the very beginning that Jimmy Carter was going to be President of the United States." One morning, Barnes and some other local politicians and lawyers were at City Café on Church Street in Marietta,

> with a long table in back and we would all meet up there in the morning unless we were off to court or something and we'd drink coffee around 7, 7:30. Al would come by, Joe Mack [Wilson], Harold Willingham, me, all of us. Al came in and read this article [Bill Shipp had written an article called "Jimmy Who?"] and everybody was laughing about Jimmy Carter going to run for President and there came a dead silence and Al says, "Well, boys, he's going to be the next President of the United States; I'm just as convinced of it as I am that I'm going to take the next breath."

Barnes found this to be "A good example of his perceptive nature—he saw something in Jimmy Carter that most people did not."[45]

As his immediate family members, from his wife and son and daughter to his sisters and brothers attest, Burruss entered public service because he believed he could make life better for others. Given his success and the esteem of his colleagues in the House—he was reelected as Speaker pro tempore in 1975 and 1976—and his having had close relationships with two governors, first Carter, then Busbee, it is understandable that Burruss would want to move upward into an even greater position of power where he could accomplish even more. But his next political move almost proved his undoing.

In 1976, he announced he would run for Speaker of the House. Though Speaker pro tempore is a powerful post, presiding over the House in the Speaker's absence, real power resides with the Speaker.[46] Arnold Fleischmann, associate professor formerly of University of Georgia, and Carol Pierannunzi, former director of the A. L. Burruss Institute of Public Service & Research, point out that "Perhaps the greatest power of the Speaker is the ability to appoint the membership of the committees that will review and draft legislation."[47] When Burruss sent out the press release announcing his intention to run for Speaker, he revealed what those who knew him best might call his combative side.

Though Burruss was generally an affable man, he "had a temper," according to his friend Chet Austin, who remembers an incident that involved the vendor that Tip Top Poultry allowed to come onsite to sell food and drinks to employees at lunch time. He said he and Al were "Careful as to who we'd allow. We'd let one get on the property who'd run an account with the employees. Another fellow decided he wanted to do it and was in the road. Al went down to convince him to leave and they got into it. Police came and put Al in the back seat and took him home. They let him go. Only thing he ever said was, 'they don't have any handles in the back of those police cars.'"[48] Of course, this incident can also be seen as one in which Burruss was protecting the rights of the vendor he was permitting to sell exclusively to the employees and perhaps protecting the employees as well if this vendor was known to offer safe food. But it's also a telling example of Burruss's sense of fairness and his willingness to assert himself when needed.

In the press release, Burruss came out swinging, claiming his mission was to create more democracy within the House, to achieve House reform, to "limit the tyrannical power of the Speaker so that everyone gets a

39

fair hearing," and to get rid of the "vindictiveness and retribution of the position."[49] He later toned down his rhetoric and said he was running a race for reform of the House, not a personal race against Tom Murphy.[50] Then, in a move obviously calculated to make his candidacy seem imminently reasonable, Burruss released a list of what he would do if elected Speaker to *The Marietta Daily Journal*, which duly printed it. If elected, he'd

> introduce a proposal to call bills and resolution for debate on the House floor according to how they appear on the general calendar; a proposal to restructure the appropriation process to "open it up" to all House members; a plan to change House rules so legislators can bring up a controversial issue a second time without interference from the Speaker; a proposal to allow House membership to elect the Democratic policy committee instead of its being appointed by the Speaker; a plan to change House rules so that a bill or resolution may only be reconsidered once.[51]

From this list it is obvious that Burruss had been chaffing under Murphy's dominance and the plans and proposals he lays out are all about fairness—about being treated with the respect and integrity owed to members of the House, and he wants this not only for himself, but also for everyone else. Burruss had noble ideas, but they showed little understanding of how politics in Georgia worked, and little sense of just how powerful Murphy really was. Judge Harris Hines, Justice of the Georgia Supreme Court, spelled out what Burruss was up against, when he said, "Now you've got to remember the speaker in the House of Representatives in Georgia here is extremely powerful. The budgetary process starts there but also the speaker basically appoints enough committee chairmen and vice-chairmen to win an election if you run against him."[52] Despite traveling throughout the summer, talking to legislators and asking for their support, when the House voted that November, Burruss lost to Murphy ninety-eight to fifty-eight.[53]

Though he might have been expected to resign as Speaker pro tempore, Burruss refused to do so, telling reporters, "I am not a quitter."[54] Of course, he was not reelected to the post in the next legislative session, nor were he and his supporters made chairs of any committees.[55] Recalling this time,

Tom Murphy later said, "I never did understand why Al wanted to become Speaker so hard, except I guess he'd always been sort of top dog in everything he ever did so he wanted to have the feeling he was top dog here. He would have been disappointed because being the speaker in this place here you've got a lot of folks you've got to listen to and you don't always necessarily get your way."[56] Though Burruss lost the election to Speaker, he managed to get some changes in the House and later earned Murphy's respect, as Murphy himself relates: "Good came out of it... I began including many more people in the decision-making process. I broadened the thing tremendously. Of course he and I became good friends. He was a very smart fellow, he was a hard worker. He had no limit he'd put on time in doing the job." Murphy had a rueful appreciation of the kind of worker Burruss was. "He was one of the hardest workers I've ever seen but when he locked in on something it was awful hard to get him to change. He didn't like to make compromises. And sometimes in this business that's what you have to do."[57] Murphy turned out to be the longest serving Speaker of the House in Georgia's history, indeed in the history of any state. According to Fleischmann and Pierannunzi, he did not face a challenge to his Speakership from the time Burruss opposed him until 1992.[58] That Burruss took him on and survived to become one of the most powerful legislators in the House says a great deal about Burruss's perseverance. As he told numerous reporters, he was not a quitter.

Jimmy Carter may have said it best about Burruss's comeback: "You know I ran for governor once and lost. For reelection for President and lost. Al was able not only to accept the defeat but to analyze the reasons for it. And then in an almost unprecedented way to come back from it. He later became as you know a leader, one of the top leaders in the House even when he had challenged the political forces that he couldn't overcome."[59] There was speculation that Burruss might go to Washington with Jimmy Carter, who had won the presidential election the same fall in which Burruss lost his own campaign, but he did not. He remained in Georgia at the state House, where he gradually rebuilt not only a position of trust, but went on to become majority whip, then majority leader, a post he held until his death.

A. L., at age two, "Sloppin' the hogs" at the Burruss home in Cumming, Georgia. (1929)

A. L. (kneeling in front, second from the right) on the honor board of Smyrna High School. Chet Austin (far right, sitting on stone column) is also in this photo. (1944)

A. L. (second from the left) as the Smyrna High School basketball team manager and timekeeper. Chet Austin (fourth from the right) is also on the team. (1944)

A. L.'s high school graduation portrait. (1944, Smyrna High School)

IMAGES

A. L. in his Navy uniform. (1944)

A. L. standing in front of a car. (1947)

Bobbi and A. L. at Thanksgiving. (1954)

A. L. holding his son, Robin. (1954)

(Below) A. L., helping distribute campaign fly swatters, talks with Buddy Darden. Although the photo was taken during Burruss's 1968 campaign, Darden signed this photo for Renée in 1987. (1968)

IMAGES

Burruss Not Elected!
Go to the Polls November 3, 1964 and Affirm your choice for Commission Post 4.

Remember His Promise to Use His Extensive Business Experience and Other God-Given Abilities to Administer the Affairs of Cobb County in an Honorable and Efficient Manner.

He Will Not Forget!
Paid For by Cobb County Democra...

AL BURRUSS
MAKES ONE PROMISE

To use my extensive business experience and other God Given abilities to administer the affairs of Cobb County in an honorable and efficient manner.

Support AL BURRUSS
FOR COMMISSION
WESTERN DISTRICT – 4 YR. TERM
ON SEPTEMBER 9th

VOTE FOR AND ELECT
AL BURRUSS

Representative
117th District
Cobb & Paulding
Counties Post 7

PROVEN EXPERIENCE!
GOVERNMENT- Member of Cobb County Commission
BUSINESS- President Tip Top Poultry, Inc.
Chairman of the Board, Cedar Valley Mills

LET EXPERIENCE WORK FOR YOU
ELECT AL BURRUSS

(Top) Campaign advertisement that ran daily for one week in October of 1964; (Middle) campaign advertisement that ran in the newspaper on August 21, 1964; and (Bottom) campaign advertisement for State Representative in 1968.

A. L. and Georgia Governor Lester Maddox stand with Cindy Penick (Guthrie), Lorrie Austin (Long), and Renée Burruss. (1969)

Wedding of Penny Owens to Robin Burruss accompanied by A. L. and Bobbi. (1970)

A. L. and Georgia Governor Jimmy Carter stand with Beth (Mauldin) Brooks, and Renée Burruss. (1972)

Letter to A. L. from the desk of Jimmy Carter. (1976)

JIMMY CARTER
November 22, 1976

To Al Burruss

I appreciate your high recommendation of Patrick Banks, and assure you that I will give every consideration to your suggestion that he be appointed to the Unemployment Compensation Commission.

Sincerely,

Jimmy Carter

JC/sc

You fought a good fight against great odds. I'm proud of you! Remember that I lost my first time in 1966.

A. L. in his office at the Georgia House of Representatives. (1974)

A. L. and Bobbi in Burruss's office at the Georgia House of Representatives on the last day of the session. (1974)

A. L. and Bobbie with Governor George Busbee and his wife, Mary Elizabeth, at the Governor's mansion in Atlanta. (1975)

A. L. and Bobbi in Burruss's office at the House. (1976)

Portrait of A. L.'s parents, Chess and Eula Burruss. (1976)

Wedding of Renée Burruss to Ken Davis accompanied by A. L. and Bobbi. (1979)

Shaking hands with the President. (L–R: John Foster, Governor George Busbee, President Jimmy Carter, Judge Clarence Vaughn, A. L. Burruss, and Hugh Carter. (Photo by Jessie Sampley, 1977)

A. L. in a discussion with Joe Mack Wilson. (1979)

A. L., Renée, Robin, and Bobbi at home on Renée's wedding day. (1979)

A. L. talks with Georgia Governor Joe Frank Harris at an early 1980s Jefferson-Jackson dinner.

IMAGES

A. L., baby Jared, Renée and Bobbi stop for a photo at Renée's graduation from Kennesaw State College. (1983)

Bobbi and A. L. during the campaign against Doug Howard. (1984)

This 1983 Burruss family portrait was used in A. L.'s campaign brochure (L–R: Jared, Renée, Ken, A. L., Ashley, Bobbi, Penny, Meghan, and Robin).

A. L. dismissing the House (a ritual of adjournment sine die). (1986)

Meet Al Burruss...

The Burruss Family: Al Burruss married Bobbi Elrod from Cornelia. Al and Bobbi have a son, Robin, a daughter, Renee Burruss Davis, and three grandchildren; all living in the Marietta area.

Al Burruss, the oldest of eleven children, was born near Cumming, in the hills of North Georgia. He has lived and worked in Cobb County since moving here in 1935.

Al believes in hard work. Al Burruss is a product of hard work. While attending elementary and high school, Al worked as a janitor, delivery boy, and on a farm.

In 1945, Al Burruss joined the United States Navy and served as a refrigeration machinist. Four years after his honorable discharge, he purchased a partnership in Tip Top Poultry Company and was later joined in this venture by his brother Jimmy, and school friend, Chet Austin. Al Burruss continues to serve as President of Tip Top Poultry, Inc.

The Burruss family is active in the First United Methodist Church of Marietta where Al serves as a member of the Administrative Board and Finance Committee, and has served on the Board of Trustees. Al serves on the Kennesaw College Foundation and has served on the Southern Tech Foundation, the Kennestone Hospital Authority, and as President of the Western Little League.

Representative Burruss began his public service career by serving as Cobb County Commissioner from 1965-1969. He followed this by being elected to the Georgia House of Representatives in 1969 where he has served for 16 years. In 1974, Burruss was elected by his colleagues as Speaker Pro-Tempore of the House. In 1980, he was elected Majority Whip. In 1982, House members elected Al as their Majority Leader.

Paid for by friends for Al Burruss.

Re-Elect

AL BURRUSS

A Champion Legislator For Cobb County

...20 Years of Service

Pages from A. L. Burruss's election brochure that was used during his last campaign for the House of Representatives. (1984)

HARD WORKING DEDICATED EXPERIENCED
AL BURRUSS
...20 Years in Public Service

Georgia Legislators are in session for only 40 days. Al Burruss works for his community twelve months of the year. He is a committed leader and worker who takes no season off from his public service responsibilities.

Al Burruss . . . a representative that makes a difference with YOU in mind.

Al Burruss . . .

A champion legislator for Cobb County . . . a champion public servant for Cobb County for 20 years . . . 4 years as a Cobb County Commissioner... 16 years in the House of Representatives serving Cobb County... Elected by his House Colleagues in 1974 as Speaker Pro-Tem. In 1980, elected as Majority Whip of the House . . . Elected to serve as House Majority Leader in 1982.

Al Burruss's ability has earned him the respect of his fellow legislators. You do not get that respect automatically by simply being elected to the House of Representatives. You have to earn it, and that takes time. Al Burruss is the Majority Leader of the House, and he also has many years of service on the following decision making committees:

- Appropriations Committee
- Ways and Means Committee
- Rules Committee
- Budget Committee
- Budget Conference Committee
- Policy Committee

Al Burruss's years as a key legislator in the House of Representatives puts him in a position to speak out **and be heard** on important issues that affect Cobb County and you.

Al Burruss brings home Cobb County's fair share of state funds and services for his constituents.

Al Burruss is the only Representative from Cobb County that has served on the Budget Conference Committee. This committee recommends the final version of the state budget.

Al Burruss . . . A Conservative and his record proves it. . .

- Author of House Bill 95 — providing more than 25 million state dollars to reduce property tax in Marietta and Cobb.

- Worked with Board of Regents to make Kennesaw College and Southern Tech 4 year institutions and has worked for increased funding for new buildings and higher percentage of Regents's budget for both institutions.

- Passed legislation that increased teacher retirement benefits and other benefits for school bus drivers and custodians.

(Left and Right) Pages from A. L. Burruss's election brochure that was used during his last campaign for the House of Representatives. (1984)

Representative Burruss is hardworking, direct, and experienced. Cobb county is better off because Al Burruss has spent twenty years representing and working for you!

Al Burruss . . . A citizen honored and respected by his community . . .

- Cobb County Citizen-of-the-Year, 1983.
- Special Appreciation Award — Association of Retarded Citizens, 1983.
- Recognition for "Outstanding Contribution" to the Cities of Georgia.
- Honorary Alumni, Kennesaw College.
- Jaycees Young Man-of-the-Year, 1962.
- Recognition for "Outstanding Service and Contribution" to the Georgia Recreation and Park Society.

- Supported every reasonable property tax relief proposal.
- Never supported any sales, income, or property tax increase of any kind unless people were given right to vote for the change. Initiated removal of sales tax from prescription drugs, eye glasses, and contact lenses.
- Worked for passage of school property tax exemptions for Cobb's senior citizens.
- Reduced income tax by increasing standard deduction for all citizens.
- Authored $2,000 exemption of retirement income (62 and older or disabled).
- Led fights that killed tax legislation harmful to Cobb and State.
- Won battles to protect Cobb's Chattahoochee River.
- Primary author and conferee of resolution to revise State Constitution.
- Secured funds for day services and new Mental Retardation Training Center in Cobb.

The Presidential candidates will be first on your ballot. Vote for your choice, then move on to the other candidates.

Be sure to vote INDIVIDUALLY FOR AL BURRUSS.

AL BURRUSS...A CLEAR WINNER

"I make only one promise . . . to continue to use my extensive business and legislative experience and other God given abilities to administer the affairs of Cobb County in an honorable and efficient manner."

Al Burruss

A.L. Burruss
Georgia House of Representatives
District 20-2

Portrait of Bobbi and A. L. (1985)

A. L., standing with Jared, Renée, and Speaker of the House Tom Murphy at the beginning of Burruss's last House session. (1986)

Jared, former President Jimmy Carter, and A. L. Burruss at the Burruss home in Marietta. (1986)

CHAPTER 4

THE SENIOR STATESMAN: IN HIS ELEMENT

After losing his position as Speaker pro tempore in the early 1970s, Al Burruss worked hard to come back to a strong position in the House. He was determined to prove that he was "not a quitter." Tom Scott describes how unusual Burruss's comeback was: "He lost all of his power for several years as a result. He was punished for having challenged the Speaker. Everybody that challenges knows that there is going to be a price to be paid. And yet I think maybe one of the most remarkable things about him was that he was able to work his way back to the leadership again and smooth it all over."[1] Fleischmann and Pierannunzi attribute Murphy's hold on the Speaker position and Burruss's loss to him as the result of "old-boy politicians."[2] In their book, *Politics in Georgia*, they remind readers that after Burruss's attempt to unseat Murphy, no one else made such a move until 1992, when DuBose Porter tried to do so, but also lost in his attempt.[3] Paul Shields attributed part of Burruss's comeback to his skills as a businessman, noting that Burruss "didn't take long to work himself back into the inner circle. After all, here was a man who had started with just a few truckloads of refrigeration equipment and transformed them into a multimillion dollar poultry processing business. Although he referred to himself as just another chicken plucker, most everyone else came to know him as Mr. Budget."[4] His friend Chet Austin also recalls Burruss's business acumen: "He was as good a businessman as I've ever known. He could grasp a situation and he could negotiate from that situation. We started with nothing to negotiate with. We were able to grow and stay in business and for a small business to stay in business is something on its own."[5] It is not surprising then that Burruss was able to reinstitute himself as one of the most powerful players in the House though it would take him several years to do so. To show that he had what it took to be a serious legislator, one who could work with the old-boy network that had kept Tom Murphy in power as Speaker, Burruss concentrated on learning as much as he could about the legislative process. He focused especially on the budget, continuing to help stall or derail legislation he did not think should be passed, and working closely with all legislators, ignoring to which political party they belonged.

According to Austin, Burruss's greatest impact was on the budget, "How far his influence reached and how valuable his input was [influenced] the budget—he probably knew it better than anybody down there." Robin Burruss gives a similar assessment of his father's application of business knowledge to the state's budget process. "What made him so effective as a legislator is he knew what it means to have to make a payroll every week and he knew what it is to have to manage a business and to manage people that make that business go. And he knew what it is to court a customer. All the skills he had to learn in business made him an effective legislator." Though Burruss lost to Murphy, he retained the respect of his colleagues in the legislature, and one in particular, Marcus Collins, stood by him after his fall from favor.

When he lost his position, Burruss also lost his office space, but Marcus Collins, who chaired the House Ways and Means Committee, of which Burruss was a member, offered him space to work in his own office, telling him "you don't have an office anymore, so you can just make my office your office."[6] Collins had a table brought in for Burruss; this was very special treatment considering there were thirty other members on the Ways and Means Committee who did not enjoy such close proximity to the chair. But Collins thought this "healing" was what was needed.[7] Moreover, Collins was Tom Murphy's best friend—the two of them hunted and fished together and were very close, so Collins's actions could only have helped Burruss in regaining Murphy's trust.[8] Burruss and Collins also made a formidable pair on the Ways and Means Committee, for, as a long-time legislative aide said, "if Marcus and Al came on the floor with anything, they got their way. So they were very powerful. I mean it was incredible."[9] However, this aide is also careful to point out that the two men did not "mandate anything. They simply expressed it in a manner that all of the people could understand."[10]

Pete Phillips, later vice chairman of Ways and Means, when nominating Burruss for majority whip at the Democratic caucus in November of 1980, argued that Burruss deserved the position partly for his commendable work on the committee:

> Al could have sulked his way through four years of House service, but he chose instead to pick himself up to not only represent his people in an excellent manner, but took the flack by killing countless bills in Ways and Means that would have caused the defeat of many House members if they had had to vote on the bills on the floor.[11]

After Burruss's death, Marcus Collins recalled that:

> Al paid his way; he worked his way. Nothing was ever given to him. And he worked hard to get back. After being defeated, he was out. He finally came back and ran for majority whip for the Democrat party and was elected and then later he ran for the majority leader. And that put him on the Conference Committee on the Budget.[12]

Joe Mack Wilson, another long-serving and powerful legislator who served with Burruss in the House, argues that Murphy's eventual embracing of Burruss was a smart move, and worked favorably for both men because Murphy "got all Al's people and became the most powerful speaker in the House. And Al won influence too."[13]

Another significant element of Burruss's comeback was that he did so on his own terms. As the legislative aide on the Ways and Means Committee explains, Burruss took his own counsel and would oppose the other 179 members of the House if he thought it was the right thing to do.[14] Moreover, Burruss kept his thoughts and plans to himself until he was ready to act on them, as he did when he cast his vote for the ERA when the rest of the House voted against it. This willingness to oppose legislation he felt was wrong happened often enough that some House staffers came to think of Burruss as being the "fly in the ointment," enough so that they presented him with a jar of ointment into which they had inserted a fly.[15] Certainly Tom Murphy found him intractable at times, though he nevertheless appreciated him. Former Governor Roy Barnes also describes Burruss as "stubborn. If he ever made up his mind, it was near impossible to change it. Now he was very open before he made up his mind, but if he ever made up his mind, boy, that was it."[16]

Even though he was considered incredibly articulate and persuasive in putting his views across, Burruss sometimes thought of his abilities as inadequate because he lacked a college education.[17] But no one who knew him ever thought of him as anything but highly capable. Judge Harris Hines once said of Burruss's ability to understand legislation: "I have seen him read legislation—he not only was a quick read, but he could understand it in depth; he could look at legislation real quick and he could go right to the heart of it."[18] Barnes also speaks highly of Burruss's capabilities, "Al was very good, he probably knew more about taxation than anybody at the Capitol."[19]

However, the qualities of Burruss that really served to reinstate him in a position of power in the House were the ones cited by Phillips in his nomination speech for Burruss to become majority whip:

- Al would assist any member by telling him what was in a bill without telling him how to vote for it.
- He never denied his skills to any member even when he disagreed with them [sic] on the issue.
- Al was familiar with losing perhaps better than anyone in the House.
- The members owed Al a formal position of leadership; he had earned it and was capable, and it was time he took his rightful place in the order of things.[20]

Burruss could be very persuasive, changing his approach depending on what was at stake. At times, he was what one person described as "calm and soft spoken and humble and benevolent.... He was very quiet and moved around the House helping with their business."[21] His son Robin says of his father's manner in dealing with others that "He told people things they didn't want to hear a lot of times politically, but he always told them the truth and he always told them what he felt was best. They always respected him knowing that what you see is what you get, and what he says is what he means."[22] Roy Barnes concurs with this assessment, that "in Al's life, it's whether a fellow sticks to his word—in legislative give and take, what's most important is that you stick to your word."[23] Burruss's rhetoric could be fiery, as noted by Hal Straus, a political writer for *The Atlanta Journal-Constitution*. He referred to Burruss as the "five-star general in Murphy's war" to strip $40 million from the Department of Transportation's budget in 1985. Straus wrote that "It was Burruss, 57, who made the angry speeches to fire up the troops and quietly convinced reluctant warriors to get to the front line."[24] Another political writer for *The Atlanta Journal-Constitution*, Frederick Allen, saw Burruss in a slightly different political role—as Tom Murphy's "prime minister."[25] As Tom Scott says, Burruss made a "remarkable comeback"—from losing his position as Speaker pro tempore to becoming majority whip, then majority leader, to becoming Murphy's right-hand man—his "five-star general," his "prime minister."

The two decades in which Burruss served in the House marked an important time because Cobb County's General Assembly delegates held sway in the legislature, unlike any time before or since. Cobb County's delegation, like the county itself, moved from being primarily composed of legislators who were Democrats in the early 1970s to becoming an increasingly bipartisan delegation in the 1980s. In his history of Cobb County politics, Tom Scott examines the changes that brought the Republicans to power in Cobb County—"a well-educated and affluent population, an important defense industry, a dramatic increase in the non-Georgia born population, and a relatively small, but affluent, minority population."[26] In his political career, Burruss only faced opposition twice from a Republican and in both instances, he defeated them. In 1970, Burruss faced opposition for his House seat from Republican Ken Nix; in the election polls from Cobb County, Burruss got 23,834 votes to Nix's 15,011 votes.[27] Burruss and Nix congratulated each other on running clean-cut campaigns. Burruss also predicted that Nix would eventually become a factor in Cobb politics,[28] a prediction that came true as Nix was elected to a seat in the House in the next election.[29] Burruss was especially pleased with the outcome of the election because of the personal endorsement he felt he received: "The people of Cobb County have convinced me that they vote for the man and not the party. If they weren't splitting tickets, Nix would be elected based on Suit."[30]

Burruss didn't face opposition again for fourteen years; in 1984, Republican Doug Howard ran against him. Unlike the earlier race against Nix, this race was ugly, with Howard running a smear campaign to undo what he called the "good old boy" network in the legislature, to which he tried to link Burruss. As Tom Sharp reported, Howard "accused Burruss of being an integral part of a 'bad government,'" rocked by scandal.[31] In an interview Burruss gave Sharp, he stressed that the committee memberships he held were based on seniority, and that "the influence he has managed to accumulate in the House holds far more potential for benefit to Cobb than anything an untried freshman could do."[32] Burruss wasn't the lone Democrat facing Republican opposition—Joe Mack Wilson and Terry Lawler were also up against Republican opponents. The editors of *The Marietta Daily Journal* recommended its readers vote for Al Burruss and Joe Mack Wilson because "the Cobb delegation has developed into the strongest and most able unit of any county in the state. We need to keep this team together."[33] Lawler was probably not included because he was seeking his second term in office and did not yet have the clout of the older legislators. Four Cobb seats in the House were in contest; the fourth was the challenge to Republican Tom Wilder by Democrat Juanelle Edwards.[34]

Bill Kinney, associate editor of *The Marietta Daily Journal*, called the race "exciting." "Never before in Cobb's political history have so many races been contested in a general election."[35] Kinney accurately predicted Wilson, Burruss, and Lawler would be reelected. Of Burruss, he said: "Like Wilson, Democrat Al Burruss is a tower of strength in the Georgia House, being majority leader. He too serves on several powerful committees and can make things happen when Cobb County needs a project. A new legislator would take years to achieve the status of Wilson and Burruss."[36] Following the election, the paper reported that the three Democratic incumbents—Wilson, Burruss, and Lawler—had faced "much stronger competition than they had expected." In the end, five Democratic incumbents were defeated by Republicans, effectively keeping the Democrats from gaining new strength in the House.[37] The Cobb delegation in the House had already been split evenly, with four Democrats and four Republicans in the 1980 election, so the 1984 election didn't change things for Cobb.[38] Partly the success of the Republican challenge was the result of gaining office on incumbent Ronald Reagan's coattails. With the advent of Ronald Reagan to the US presidency, as Scott explains, "Cobb Republicans surged ahead of their rivals, becoming in the 1980s virtually as powerful as the Democrats had been a few years earlier."[39] Burruss won 56.8 percent of the Cobb County vote in the 1984 election.[40]

While working to regain his standing in the House during the mid- to late-1970s, Burruss also supported Jimmy Carter in his run for the US presidency—he and his wife Bobbi and his brother Gerald were part of the Peanut Brigade and actively campaigned for Carter in New Hampshire for the first primary held in February, 1976. They were among the ninety Georgians who showed up to walk the streets, handing out literature and telling people about Jimmy Carter.[41] The next January, the Burruss family found themselves at the Carter inauguration, standing in the snow as Carter was sworn in as the thirty-ninth US president.[42] Burruss and his wife Bobbi were often guests of the Carters at the White House during Carter's term in office. Al Burruss worked behind the scenes to support Carter's work as well. For example, when the Panama Canal treaties were being decided upon in Congress, Burruss was among a group of twenty-two Georgians who traveled to Washington, DC, for state briefings on the Panama Canal Treaty at the White House on August 30, 1977.[43] Although exactly what Burruss's role was in supporting Carter is unclear, beyond attending functions, there are letters sent from the White House, thanking him for his support and enlisting his aid in supporting the treaties.

Three letters sent to Burruss specifically mention the Panama Canal Treaties; the first was sent by Hamilton Jordan, assistant to the president, dated October 6, 1977, which thanks Burruss "for joining us here at the White House for the briefing" and requesting Burruss's "full and public support of them"; also enclosed were the texts of the two treaties on the Panama Canal, signed in Washington, September 7, 1977.[44] The second letter was sent by Betty Rainwater, deputy assistant to the president for research, dated November 17, 1977, explaining that "President Carter asked me to pass on to you, because of your interest in the Panama Canal Treaties, the enclosed material"; enclosed were recent news articles and public opinion survey results related to the Panama Canal Treaties.[45] A final letter was sent by Jimmy Carter himself, though it appears to be a form letter, not a personal letter, signed with a large "J" that thanks Burruss for the "active interest that you and many other Americans took in this vital issue," and ending with the injunction from the president, "I hope you will continue to let your voice be heard on other issues in the future."[46] Whether or not Burruss did participate again in public issues is unclear. Yet, he was considered a warm friend and often invited to stay at the White House with Bobbi and attend functions such as a barbecue on the South Lawn.[47] One question that comes up is why Burruss didn't accompany Carter to Washington—was he not asked or did he not want to go? According to Rachel Fowler, Burruss's secretary, "He could have gone very definitely to Washington. He considered running for Congress but he didn't want to raise his children in Washington." His family also agree that Burruss had only to say the word and he could have been in Washington, but he provided a humorous explanation when asked about why he didn't go: "Chickens don't like cold weather."

In the 1980 elections, House majority whip Nathan Knight was defeated by Republican Neal Shepard; this opened up the position and Burruss announced early on that he intended to run for it.[48] Elected by the Democratic caucus in November of 1980 to the post of majority whip, Burruss became, if possible, even more visible in the power structure of the House. The majority whip "assist[s] the majority leader by keeping members advised of floor and committee votes," "deliver[s] the necessary amount of votes needed on particular pieces of legislation favored by the majority party," and "manages the legislative agenda of the party."[49] During 1981's General Assembly session, Burruss was named to the House committee overseeing the revision of Georgia's constitution, was vice chairman of the Rules Committee, and served on the State Regulatory Agency, Ways and Means, and Appropriations Committees.[50] He was constantly moving about the House, talking with its representatives, lining up votes, persuading, cajoling, and when necessary, using stronger measures. He was especially good at persuading people to accept his views, as demonstrated by Carter's recollection of how Burruss could influence people:

> When somebody would have a very negative comment to make or made a speech that was highly damaging to what we were trying to do, Al had a way to put out fires and to calm a difficult situation down, whereas someone with less sensitivity to human beings, with less confidence in himself would have probably aggravated an already bad situation and made more enemies. But he knew how to turn an enemy into a friend. He learned how to turn an antagonist into a supporter.[51]

A legislative aide remembers watching Burruss work the floor of the House: "Al was just such an incredible leader, and he did it not just by leading the body but by leading them one by one, helping them, showing them, taking their legislation and proving it; that's how he did it. It was a sight to behold."[52] As in everything he did, Burruss took his job to heart and spent many hours supporting the goals of his party and of his constituents, using his committee memberships to get legislation through the House.

The real work of the House takes place in the committees, where members decide on the value of the legislation under consideration—whether it needs more study, should go forward, or not be acted on further.[53] Thus, Burruss's committee memberships indicate both his stature in the House, as well as his ability to influence legislation. In 1982, another opportunity opened up for Burruss and he ran for majority leader, which he easily won. As majority leader, Burruss was "responsible for leading the floor debate on majority-party issues and for insuring that Democratic votes fall where leaders want them to."[54] By being elected majority leader, Burruss automatically gained seats on the three most powerful House committees: Ways and Means, Rules, and Appropriations.[55]

These three committees were, and continue to be, powerful because they largely determine the way legislation moves through the House. As Fleishmann and Pierannunzi explain, the Rules Committee meets daily during the last twenty days of the session to determine which bills will be discussed on the floor that day, with the consequence that: "the Rules

Committee may decide that a particular piece of legislation is never acted upon by the House, even if the standing committee favors it. Members of the Rules Committee therefore hold substantial power over all legislation."[56] Moreover, the chairs of this committee in both chambers "are strong political forces in the General Assembly, as little legislation that does not meet their approval is likely to be passed."[57] The Appropriations Committee holds hearings on the governor's Amended General Budget Report proposal the week before the General Assembly session convenes and reviews the budget (within its subcommittees) for policy areas such as education, higher education, public safety, and so on.[58] So, this, too, was a powerful committee that Burruss served on. According to Roy Barnes, Burruss used his power, when necessary, to get legislation passed. "Al had a tough streak in him, too. If needed to be, Al could be tough to get his point across. I've seen him punish legislators that voted against him—punished them hard, took everything they had out of the budget and wouldn't let their bill out of the committee."

Former State Representative Tom Kilgore describes what Burruss was like as majority leader: "The job of the majority leader is to explain the budget. He had to know that budget, every figure, everything had to be just so. He would come in before he was to explain it to a committee, to the full House, or to anybody, and we'd sit down and we'd go over that thing for hours on end, me picking him and asking questions that anyone might ask him. His greatest fear in politics was that somebody would ask him a question and he could not answer it."[59] Kilgore also remembered the way in which Burruss helped other legislators.

> If you got in trouble, didn't matter whether you were friend or foe, didn't make any difference whether he agreed or disagreed on a piece of legislation, whether he was going to vote for or against it, didn't matter. If you got in trouble, he rescued you. You knew he was like a life preserver sitting here. And he would throw out a question or he would clear his throat or do something to give you time to develop an answer and get yourself out of that problem.[60]

Joe Mack Wilson also stressed Burruss's trait of helpfulness as a major difference between him and other majority leaders.

> Al was not your typical majority leader; first of all he was more than a majority leader, he was a father figure to some of those youngsters. They sought him out and formed lines to get into his office, seeking advice on everything from the price of chicken to how we gonna handle this next bill. And so he was not an ordinary majority leader.[61]

At a time when the legislature was slowly being integrated, and many in the House were not very progressive in their thinking, Burruss knew no color limits—he was as helpful to the Congressional Black Caucus and the black representatives as to any others. A legislative aide claimed that "He treated them just like he did the white members as far as working with their legislation and helping them with their legislation in every way he could. He treated them no differently than the white members of the House, that's for sure. His professional attitude [was] 'they're a member of the House representing a state the same as I do.'"[62] Representative Eleanor Richardson also remembered how Burruss showed great "concern for women and children and health issues. In his position of handling the money and being on rules and being on all these important committees, he really helped me tremendously."[63] In 1985, for example, Burruss and Wilson saw to it that $73,000 were earmarked in the budget for the Open Gate shelter for abused children in Cobb County.[64] The two representatives also sponsored a bill to increase the exemption of retirement benefits from state income taxes, for, as Burruss said, "This is one of my priorities. I feel we have to do something for people on fixed incomes to offset the increased cost of living."[65] Roy Barnes later said of his friend, "Al had a philosophy that was really born out of rural Forsyth County. Hard work, always make sure that you treat your fellow man with equality, make sure that you are never called into question on anything that you do publicly or that you do privately. And upon his death I could truly say that I look back at Al Burruss's life and it was one that was unblemished. All of us have skeletons but he had very, very few."

One legislator, former State Representative Terry Lawler, tells how Burruss mentored him during his early legislative career. Burruss met Lawler when he was working for the General Assembly in the House chamber. Burruss encouraged him to run for representative, saying that even though he might not win the first time, he should keep running. Lawler did run, unsuccessfully at first in 1978, but then he gained a seat in 1980. For his first year in the House, Burruss told Lawler to listen, not speak, and he would hear others ask the questions he was thinking. Lawler took Burruss's advice and from him learned the ins and outs of how to get legislation passed in the House, primarily by getting an amendment attached to someone else's bill. Lawler points out that even though Burruss's name appears on many bills, a lot of what he accomplished was in amendments to someone else's bill.[66]

Burruss was the newly elected majority leader in the House when Governor Joe Frank Harris took office in 1983. Roy Barnes, Governor Harris's floor leader in the Senate, introduced the newly established Education Review Commission and Al Burruss was appointed to the commission as well. The commission came up with the concept of Quality Basic Education (QBE), the funding mechanism Georgia still operates under today. Improving education was an idea that Burruss could wholly support. In an interview with Bill Carbine, a political writer for *The Atlanta Journal-Constitution*, Burruss brought up his own educational background stated that, "One thing my Dad did... is that he said that his children could not get a basic education in Forsyth County so he brought us to Smyrna when I was 7. If it had not been for that move I would be a textile worker or something today."[67] One of the primary issues facing the General Assembly in 1984 was financing public education, and Burruss saw education as the key to solving a lot of social problems. He said "If we can solve that one thing [a way to finance minimal basic education]we can solve a lot of other problems, unemployment, prison problems, crime problems, and we can bring new industry to Georgia."[68] But, he was not in favor of issuing bonds to pay for it; as he said, "I've never been able to get out of debt by borrowing."[69]

When the Education Review Commission published its report, in November of 1984, one of its more controversial features was opposed by Burruss. The commission had proposed a formula by which the state would steer more of the new money toward poor school districts; at that time, school districts were funded by property taxes, which favored wealthier counties. But Burruss expressed skepticism of the commission's recommendation for equalizing school finance,"It appears to me it will penalize the good systems where taxpayers have been willing to pay the necessary cost of a quality education."[70] On the other hand, he favored the recommendation of teacher accountability and the establishment of a career ladder for teachers with steps to improve their pay and performance.[71] Burruss pushed hard to get the education reform bill through the House though it would take two years to do so. In 1985, the House approved the state budget, leaving education reform intact, and the school reform bill finally passed in the House on February 23, 1985. The bill established a mandatory full-day kindergarten,[72] something Burruss had fought for when George Busbee was governor, but they could not get it through the legislature ten years earlier.[73] Political writer Frederick Allen called the education reform bill "the most revolutionary reform of the public schools in Georgia history."[74]

Another important piece of legislation that Burruss and Barnes worked on together, along with Joe Mack Wilson, was the 1 percent local option sales tax that could be used for road improvements and other such projects by the counties. This bill was the product of a brainstorming session that Burruss and Wilson had with Roy Barnes and is an example of how legislation sometimes works. Barnes related the story about how this bill came about:

> Al and I went to the First United Methodist Church together and after services, I would go over and work a few hours at my office up the street. Al and Joe Mack came over and said Earl Smith had come to them and needed money for county roads and bridges. [Smith] was the first Republican chair of the Cobb County Commission, which shows cooperation across party lines. So Joe Mack and Al said they wanted to know how to do a local option sales tax.[75]

So Barnes pulled his code and, working over the next three hours, they wrote the bill out in longhand. The next morning, "Al took it to Legislative Council. Al and Joe Mack introduced the bill in the House and it was tough but it passed. [Barnes] had an easier time in the Senate but there were some amendments placed on the bill. When it came back to the House for agreement to the Senate amendments, Al asked [Barnes] to come over and help him work the floor and [he] did. It passed the House with only one vote to spare. It was a monumental achievement and only Al could have pulled it off." As Barnes recalls:

> It was close. Historically we had said no local government could impose a local sales tax because the sales tax was solely the state's. This went back to the time when Herman Talmadge was Governor and the first sales tax was put into effect in 1951 [...], so a lot of the older legislators who remembered this… thought it was going back on what had been done 30 years before. And the argument was that the state schools are going to need expanding and when they need that taxing capacity if you give it up now, you're not going to be able to use it. That was the big argument with them.[76]

But Republican State Representative Johnny Isakson helped them and they got it passed in Cobb. Barnes noted that, "We all went to the highway board and went to Tom Moreland, who was Highway Commissioner at the time, and he said if you pass this, I'll match every dollar that y'all raise so you can get transportation money. And we did and we used it very effectively." Tom Scott, speaking about the 1 percent sales tax, said that: "In that interview that I did with Joe Mack Wilson, he talks a lot about the 1 percent sales tax. It's really important, and it's really kind of a new idea in Georgia to have that local option to build roads. And so [Wilson and Burruss] did push that through; it's a big achievement... it's what we call SPLOST [special purpose local option sales tax] nowadays."[77]

Paul Shields remarked, in the video *A Remembrance of Al Burruss*, that "Burruss had left his mark on our state constitution, our tax laws, and our educational system. But his lasting legacy is the choice that Georgians now have to tax themselves to build needed libraries, schools, and roads."[78] Barnes, too, extolled Burruss's actions in state government:

> The special option sales tax was right at the top of the list as one of Al Burruss's greatest achievements. But one of the other things that not many people know about is that Al had a driving hand in creating the funding mechanism, the funding formula for the university system, which we

still use, and to make sure that there was an equality of funds through all of the university system and to make sure that universities and colleges didn't get funded just by who happened to be the local politician in the General Assembly at the time.[79]

Not only was the 1 percent sales tax bill highly regarded by legislators, but it was entered into the competition sponsored by the Ford Foundation and Harvard's John F. Kennedy School of Government, a high honor.[80] Political writer Bill Shipp noted that,

> Not only in the Cobb County delegation but also in the suburbs around Atlanta, [Burruss] marked the bridge between the rural and the suburban legislator. [...] It was Al who was one of the founding members of the special tax districts that allowed certain urban areas to work on their infrastructure, to relieve traffic problems, that kind of thing. And that turned into a major way suburban Atlanta is coping with its growth.[81]

During the 1985 and 1986 legislative sessions, Burruss and Wilson saw to it that funds were kept in the state budgets for Kennesaw State College and Southern Tech, including "$1.2 million for land acquisition at Kennesaw... and $9 million for a new business school at Kennesaw."[82] The Coles College of Business at Kennesaw State University is now housed in the Burruss Building, named for the legislator that secured its funding. This period of the early-to mid-1980s marked a time in the Georgia General Assembly when the Cobb delegation was at its strongest and most powerful—Burruss was the House majority leader, Joe Mack Wilson was chair of the Ways and Means Committee, Roy Barnes was Governor Harris's floor leader in the Senate, and Republicans dominated the Cobb legislative delegation, holding eight of the fourteen seats, led by House minority leader Johnny Isakson.[83] According to *The Marietta Daily Journal*, old-time Georgia political observers often called the Cobb delegation "the most powerful delegation in state history."[84] Of this time, Barnes says, "I've never seen a delegation like it before or since and it was just that one period of time when if we all got together there was just nothing that couldn't be done.... We had different politics but we worked well together and we had a common love and concern for the people of Cobb County."[85] Terry Lawler expresses a similar point of view:

> Al was in the Cobb delegation at a time when it held sway in Georgia politics. It was a unique moment in Georgia history and lasted over the decade of the 1980s. Powerful men from Cobb County and its neighbors Paulding and Bartow Counties could get just about any legislation they wanted through the legislature: Joe Frank Harris from Cartersville, who would be governor during much of this decade; Joe Mack Wilson, Al Burruss, state representatives from Cobb County; Roy Barnes (whom Al referred to as the "smartest man I know"), senator from Cobb; and many others.[86]

One thing that not many know about Al Burruss was that he was a Certified Lay Speaker of the Methodist Church and regularly spoke in churches and conducted services on Laity Sunday. His faith is also reflected in another aspect of his character that not many know of—his generosity to those who were poor. One of many examples of this is related by a legislative aide in the House who remembers a day when a group of legislators and aides were eating at the Stadium Hotel and Burruss left a $200 tip for a waitress who limped while serving them. Another time, the group had eaten one night, and as they left to head for their cars, they noticed that Burruss had stopped to talk to a homeless man on the street to whom he gave a "wad of money." He was also very generous to those who worked at the House; an aide noted that "On Easter he would bring a potted flower of some sort to every female in the Capitol. There were probably 30." But he did so even when the staff increased to sixty people. He also brought chickens for all the staff at Christmas. Of his generosity, the aide said that with Burruss, "It was a constant giveaway, whether it be money or food," and for many of the women who worked at the House and made very little money doing so, his gift of chicken was often the only food they had over the holidays.[87]

Just as he was generous with what he could give people in terms of money, he was generous of his time, especially to the people of Cobb county.

For example, he donated his time, as his legislative aide said, "to all the people who could not come forth and take care of their own business under the state organization. If someone needed something in the Department of Natural Resources, perhaps a creek was flooding their back yard, Al could step in as an elected person and help iron the problem out for the person that owned the home that was being flooded by the creek.[88]" He was not only a talented businessman, but he was also "talented in working with the general public and doing all the things that needed to be done that people could not get done for themselves. And that was one of the important things that he constantly did. While he was helping all of the members of the House with their legislation, he was helping individuals with problems they had with the state that needed someone who was elected because the elected voice has the strongest voice because the people have chosen him to speak for them."[89]

Most amazing of all was that he maintained his brisk schedule: working late into the night on legislation, then up early in the morning to get the kids off to school, then dealing with all the myriad things he had to do, suffering all the while from excruciating pain from arthritis. In fact, many of the pictures that appeared in newspapers show Burruss kneeling beside a representative to discuss legislation or with his chin on his desk because that was the only way he could get relief from the constant pain. Numerous people recall how at committee meetings, he would have to lie on the floor in an attempt to get relief. His wife Bobbi thinks that one reason he didn't get much sleep was that it was too painful to be in one position. Representative Eleanor Richardson describes what it was like to witness Burruss's pain: "Al's arthritis pain—I will never forget that real courage and endurance of deep, deep pain. Because he didn't want to take too much medication because then he wouldn't be able to help the rest of us."[90]

Shortly after the General Assembly of 1986 ended, Al Burruss checked into Kennestone Hospital in Marietta for surgery to relieve what was believed to be an infected appendix. On March 9, 1986, *The Atlanta Journal-Constitution* announced in its Sunday paper that Burruss had been diagnosed with advanced pancreatic cancer.[91] The legacy of a great man was about to come to a close.

CHAPTER 5

CONCLUSION: A. L. BURRUSS, JULY 3, 1927–MAY 10, 1986

> Boys, it's a great life.
>
> —Al Burruss to Roy Barnes and friends

These are the words that Al Burruss spoke to former Governor Roy Barnes and other friends visiting him in the hospital after he had learned he had advanced pancreatic cancer. And these words pretty well sum up how Burruss felt about life—it was enjoyable, it was fun, and it was joyful. And this was not because he was a wealthy man, though that was a part of it, but he had enjoyed more than one kind of wealth in his life. Spending money when you have it can be fun, but that wasn't Burruss's idea of having fun with money. His idea was to give it away, to give away as much of it as he could, as fast as he could. Burruss's quality of giving was what Rev. Charles Sineath chose to focus on when he gave his eulogy at Burruss's funeral. As Rev. Sineath explained, Burruss gave money away because he believed God had given it to him and therefore it was his duty to share the wealth—not for his own personal glory but for the glory of God. According to Rev. Sineath, "He'd say, 'Whenever there's a special need, let me know,' and I did. I'd drop him a note, and he'd call up and ask how much was needed. He loved to give. Some people would give, but they didn't love it. He'd thank me for calling."[1] As many people said after his death, most of Burruss's giving had been done anonymously. He gave to people at his church with special needs and to the children of friends in trouble—a teenager who wrecked her car and needed money to repair it and the son of a friend who needed money to meet his mortgage or face foreclosure. He shared his wealth with people he worked with at the state House or who worked for him at Tip Top Poultry Inc. and to fellow politicians who needed help with campaign debts—US Representative Buddy Darden said Burruss helped him after his loss in 1976. He supported local organizations and Little League teams and an orphanage—the Calvary Home for Children. Burruss's generosity spread to countless homeless people—a man pushing a grocery cart while collecting cans alongside the road to sell—and to those with whom he came in contact with casually—a waitress with a limp for whom he left a $200 tip. When his friends recall his generosity, however, money is only one of the things they speak about.

Another thing Burruss had shared was his time. His wife Bobbi says he always had time for anyone who came to him for help or advice or just to talk. No one was ever turned away. If a constituent came to him with a problem, Burruss felt it his duty to help get that problem fixed if he could. His colleagues in the Georgia General Assembly say the same thing. If ever a legislator needed help, Burruss was there to discuss the legislation, answer questions, or even ask tough questions to direct the legislator in the right direction. He seemed to have boundless time and energy—one legislator said Burruss would work twenty-six hours a day if that's what it took. His wife was fond of saying, where other people had seven days a week, Al seemed to have eight. Acknowledging the enormous amount of time Al devoted to helping others, four of his fellow legislators in the House wrote to the political writer Frederick Allen to say, "Al spends a giant portion of his time helping anyone who seeks his counsel."[2] And he did all this while suffering intense arthritic pain—the kind of pain that prostrated him, causing him to lie down on the floor during committee meetings. Even when his as-yet-undetected cancer was giving him additional pain during the last session of his career, he worked eighteen-hour days, then took work home.

Fixing problems and straightening out legislators seemed second nature to him. He had, as his colleagues and friends claim, prodigious knowledge that he put to use for the people of Cobb and Paulding Counties and for the people of Georgia in general. He was known as "Mr. Budget" because he knew not only how the budget worked, but how to make it work when no one else knew quite what to do. House Speaker Tom Murphy called Burruss "one of the most intelligent, hardest working individuals I ever served with.... You could say that Al Burruss, as much as anybody, was responsible for the state of Georgia's fiscal soundness."[3] And Cobb County, his colleagues claim, reaped millions of dollars for its colleges—Kennesaw State University (formerly Kennesaw State College) and Southern Polytechnic State University (formerly Southern Technical Institute)—as well as funds for numerous local projects that Burruss personally lobbied for every year, including such things as mental retardation service programs in Cobb.[4] He knew the official legislative rules almost by heart and always carried the Rules book wherever he went in the House. He was considered the expert on state taxation—Roy Barnes said no one knew taxation like Al did.

Looking back at Burruss's life from the vantage point of more than twenty years, we see an extraordinary man. One who grew up during the hard times of the Depression and who embraced hard work in order to help support his family of nine siblings while getting his own high school education. No work was beneath him—he worked at whatever jobs were available and gave them his all. Like many another American teens during World War II, he eagerly joined the Navy, which rewarded him with the kind of training that would make life different for him and his family stateside. Burruss took the opportunities that he himself eagerly sought and made the most of them. That he was also blessed with loving friends and family and was a friendly, likeable man, helped bring him opportunities that not everyone gets or can take advantage of in the ways he did.

The things that mattered most to him—such as helping out others, be they family, friends, or strangers—were part of the driving force that fueled his ambition. But he wanted to do more than become a wealthy man—though his business acumen led to that. He wanted to be where the action was, to make it possible for people to have and lead better lives. Though he could and did give away a lot of his personal monetary wealth to the less fortunate, Burruss was more interested in giving back to others through positive action. And he never could stay still; it was as if he knew he would not have a long life in which to get all the things done that mattered to him, so he worked in overdrive. His desire to improve the conditions of others and make government responsible to the people led him into the Cobb County Commission and then into the state legislature. He learned early on that power was necessary to effect his plans of making life better for the people of Georgia.

Unlike the old-boy network he ultimately worked his way into, Burruss refused to wait for his time to come, but instead made things happen in his own time. A perfect example is when he wanted to become Speaker pro tempore and so he drove around the state garnering support, something no one had done before. When he challenged Murphy to the powerful Speaker post, he was driven by his own belief that government could be done better and that he could be the one to make changes. Even in the face of his defeat, he did not give up but fought to get back in the good graces of the powerful House network. That he did so is testament to his extraordinary work ethic and ability to make friends and keep them.

Whenever anyone talks about Burruss, even in the decades since his death in 1986, they never fail to bring up his loss to Murphy and express admiration for his extraordinary comeback in politics. It took more than hard work for Burruss to reinstate himself in the good graces of Murphy and others; the key to his comeback lay in his own personality. Burruss was genuine in his friendships and generous to his colleagues, someone to go to for sound advice and help with any problem, be it legislative or not. His integrity and honesty drew people to him and assured them that he could be trusted. Surprisingly, he was well-liked in spite of his propensity to say what he felt about any issue. As numerous people attest, Burruss always told people what he thought, what the facts were as he understood them, regardless of how people would take such information. He was honest, as some might say, to a fault. Bill Kinney, associate editor of *The Marietta Daily Journal*, wrote this when Burruss was in the house:

> His integrity was beyond question. Newsmen will tell you Al leveled with them. He felt comfortable and tuned-in with anyone, ranging from a laborer to former President Jimmy Carter. Though a millionaire, he never forgot his humble upbringing in the Georgia mountains.[5]

Though he always listened to others, he kept his own counsel and voted his own conscience. As his friends in the legislature point out, he could be stubborn—once he made up his mind there was no changing it. Yet, he was a man of contradictory traits—known for being tough yet gentle at the same time, as Lieutenant Governor Zell Miller characterized him.[6] Tough, because he was determined to get legislation passed that he believed in. Gentle, because he understood people and knew what it was like to be on the losing side. As all who knew him are quick to say of him, Al Burruss was a compassionate man. He was also a loving man, especially when it came to his family.

Early morning was the time he spent with his children, cooking their breakfast and catching up on their lives. He rarely missed a practice of his son's or daughter's while they were growing up and participating in the usual sports and other activities of middle class families. There was always time to take his wife and children on vacations, including flying his son and his high school friends to the Caribbean for diving trips or flying his family to their summer home in South Carolina. He enjoyed a game of golf when time permitted. He did all the things that people do in the course of their lives. If his life seemed richer, it was because he never sat still, waiting for life to happen—he made things happen. He grew a successful business; he joined organizations that furthered his professional aims; he got to know people from all walks of life and many of those people helped him achieve his goals, but they did so because they saw he was a good man, a man to trust. He did not serve others for personal acclaim and because he wanted to praise God, to give back because he felt that God had so blessed him, he in turn gave the same to the people he met, worked with, played with, and loved.

In his eulogy at Burruss's funeral, Rev. Sineath quoted the following passage from the book of Mark (Mark 10: 43–45), in which Jesus is addressing the disciples:

> But it is not so among you; but whoever wishes to become great among you must be your servant, and whoever wishes to be first among you must be slave of all. For the Son of Man came not to be served but to serve, and to give his life a ransom for many.[7]

Bill Kinney, describing the funeral in *The Marietta Daily Journal*, thought this passage from Mark aptly typified Burruss's life. Burruss saw himself as a servant of God first, and a servant of men second. When he lay dying, Burruss told his family and friends that he wanted, "a service of thanksgiving to the glory of God, not to Al Burruss."[8] To this end, there were twenty-nine wreaths of brightly colored flowers decorating the church's pulpit[9] at his funeral, and his family members dressed accordingly, in what his daughter Renée Burruss Davis described as "bright, triumph colors dedicated to the glory of God," rather than traditional dark colors.[10] According to Rev. Sineath, Burruss kept a message taped inside his briefcase: "God is greater than any problem I have."[11] Al Burruss put his faith into practice and for that reason, his political record and personal success need to be seen alongside that faith.

The 1986 legislative session ended on March 8; Burruss gathered up his paperwork and left the Capitol to return home in preparation for surgery to discover the source of his stomach pain. Two days later, he underwent exploratory surgery at Kennestone Hospital in Marietta, during which surgeons determined he had advanced pancreatic cancer. Doctors told him he had about sixty days to live; he died on May 10, 1986 at 7:00 a.m., with his wife Bobbi at his side. In the short time between March and May of that year, Burruss worked to get his estate in order and arrange for his son to take over as president of Tip Top Poultry, where Robin had been working since 1973. During this time, Marietta city officials named a forty-six-acre park, then being constructed at the corner of Cobb Parkway and South Cobb Drive, for Burruss, who had been instrumental in helping the city get funds to build the park; they named the park the A. L. Burruss Nature Park.[12] Today the park is a lovely natural wooded area with trails.

Before he became ill, Burruss had been scheduled to speak at the First United Methodist Church of Marietta's annual Lenten Lunch Lift in March. When he realized he would not be able to attend and speak, he recorded a message from his hospital bed that was played to the large crowd who attended the service, including some family members—his mother Eula Burruss, brother Gerald Burruss, sister Betty Brown, daughter Renée Burruss Davis, and son Robin Burruss. His wife Bobbi remained at the hospital. His message is primarily a testament of his faith (see Appendix A for the complete transcript of this recording), yet he makes it clear that death holds no fear for him.

> Since the news has come that I have pancreatic cancer that is most probably terminal, I've been strangely calm and sustained. I give all the credit for this to the fact that my faith was there stronger than even I believed it to be. I am not panicked.[13]

Barnes remembers this aspect of Burruss, "There's many people that teach us how to live. But Al Burruss taught me and others how to die. He was one of the most courageous fellows I have ever met in death."[14]

Burruss did get to go home for a short while and *The Marietta Daily Journal* reported that "He was glimpsed doing two of his favorite activities—cleaning his pool and soaking up some sunshine in a lounge chair on an 80-degree day."[15] Jimmy and Rosalynn Carter also visited him in his Marietta home one day. There weren't too many good days like these, and he had to return to the hospital. While in the hospital, however, the man who called himself a "simple chicken plucker" had many visitors[16]—national, state, and local officials, and many friends. According to his nurse, he was resting comfortably when he died.

As might be expected of such a well-loved and well-respected man, his funeral was quite large—over one thousand five hundred people attended the service at First United Methodist Church of Marietta. His two pastors, Rev. Hugh Cauthen of Mt. Zion United Methodist Church in East Cobb and Rev. Charles Sineath of First United Methodist Church of Marietta, led the service. Speaker Tom Murphy and many other state legislators sat in the choir loft and formed an honor guard for Burruss's casket as it was placed in the hearse for his burial at Kennesaw Memorial Park Cemetery. During the service, a simple beige cloth covered the casket, but this was replaced with an American flag before being placed in the hearse. Former President Jimmy Carter and Rosalynn Carter attended the funeral, as did Governor Harris, Lieutenant Governor Zell Miller, and US Representative Buddy Darden, among many others. Besides some one hundred fifty members of his family and friends in attendance, including

Chet Austin and his wife Hazel, Judge Hines and his wife Helen, six longtime employees attended, including his gardener, Howard Zachary.[17]

During his lifetime, Burruss had received many honors due to his civic and political activities. These honors continued after his death. Named in his honor, the Burruss Correctional Training Center, in Forsyth, Georgia was dedicated on Tuesday, January 20,1987. The dedication letter reads,

> The Burruss Correctional Training Center, a 300-man medium security institution, will serve as the labor component of the new Georgia Public Training Center and will house a Special Alternative Incarceration Unit. This highly regimented program for younger offenders has gained national attention during the past 2 years.[18]

In 1987, plans to create an institute of public service at Kennesaw State College to honor Burruss were announced.[19] According to Richard Hardin, a consultant for the institute,

> its purposes would be "to provide people who are interested in government and political activity with a forum and a training ground, and to serve as an information center for people who need some kind of government assistance but don't know how to get things done in government; the institute will try to help people the way he did."[20]

The A. L. Burruss Institute of Public Service & Research, was officially created by the Board of Regents of the University System of Georgia, in July of 1988. The institutes website indicates that,

> To achieve the University President's goal of "commitment to community," the Institute embarked on an ambitious plan to reach city, county, regional, state, and federal agencies and elected officials, as well as non-profit and community service organizations, by providing technical assistance and applied research services in a diversity of areas ranging from gerontology to lake management studies within North Atlanta and Northwest Georgia.[21]

Chapter 5: Conclusion: A. L. Burruss, July 3, 1927–May 10, 1986

Kennesaw State University President Emeritus Betty L. Siegel, in recalling her friend Al Burruss, thought the institute would be an ideal way to honor his memory.

> My favorite story of Al personally was when he came to my house and sat and talked with a number of students. And as he talked to the students they were all gathered around him as he sat in a chair and he was talking about what brought him into public service. He felt that God had been good to him and that he had to give something back to the community in exchange for all the blessings he had had. Al would have liked the [A. L. Burruss Institute], a continuation of what he really believed in, what he wanted to do with his life. It's a living testimony to the kinds of things that can be done in teaching, in service, and in applied research. It manifests his spirit in the best sense of the word.[22]

In 1988 The Marietta City School District dedicated an elementary school in his honor—the A. L. Burruss Elementary School. In 1991, the one hundred thousand-square-foot A. L. Burruss Building opened; it houses the Kennesaw State University Coles College of Business. The building was named for Burruss because he was instrumental in securing funding for it in the state budget.

The legacy of A. L. Burruss lives on in the institute that bears his name, and in the other places named in his honor. The heart of the man, however, lives on in the memories still held by his friends and family. This book cannot tell the whole story of who Al Burruss was—no book could do that—but it serves to remind people that here was a great man, a man who loved his state and its people, loved his family and friends, and loved his God. He still serves as an exemplar of what public service is all about and how best to do it. According to Joe Mack Wilson, Al's friend Otis Brumby, publisher of *The Marietta Daily Journal*, was fond of saying, "Al is in politics for all the right reasons."[23] A. L. Burruss was, in every instance, be it politics, church, or relationships, living life to the fullest and passionately committed for all the right reasons. His life is a lesson to us all. Roy Barnes remembers what Burruss told him one day when he visited his friend in the hospital:

> He said, 'Don't worry about me, I've had a great life.' And until the day he died he was as happy as I've ever seen him. I went to see him in the hospital when he was lingering, right at the end. I sat in there with him and he was going in and out of consciousness. And he became conscious and he said, 'Boys, it's a great life.' And those were the last words I ever heard him speak.[24]

What Burruss is remembered for is not his wealth, but his love for others, his compassion, his generosity, but most of all, as a man whose life was dedicated to public service—to making life better for all Georgians.

A. L. Burruss Chronology

1927 (Jun 3)	Born in rural Forsyth County
1934-1935	Burruss family moves to Smyrna, Georgia
1944	Graduates from Smyrna High School
1945	Enlists in US Naval Reserve; stationed in the Philippines
1947 (Aug 17)	Marries Barbara Nelle Elrod (Bobbi); they move to Smyrna, Georgia
1951	Acquires Tip Top Poultry in Marietta, Georgia, and becomes its president
1952 (Feb 5)	Son Robin Alan born
1955 (Apr 16)	Son Michael Adair born (died June 28, 1956)
1958 (Dec 10)	Daughter Patricia Renée born
1959	Moves with his family to Marietta, Georgia
1963 (Jan)	Named Area Young Man of the Year by the Jaycees
1964 (Nov 4)	Elected to Cobb County's new five-member county commission for a 4-year term beginning January 2, 1965
1968 (Apr 7)	Announces he will not run for a second term on the Cobb County Commission
1968 (Sep 11)	Wins the Democratic primary election for Post 7 in the Georgia House of Representatives
1968 (Nov 5)	Elected to the Georgia House of Representatives, the first of nine successive terms
1966	Befriends Jimmy Carter, flying him around Georgia in Carter's first, unsuccessful campaign for governor
1970	Active in Carter's second and successful campaign for governor, again loaning Carter his plane to campaign around Georgia

1971 (Jan)	Becomes Governor Jimmy Carter's administrative floor leader in the House
1974 (Jan 7)	Elected Speaker pro tempore of the Georgia House of Representatives
1975 (Jan 13)	Reelected Speaker pro tempore
1975 (May)	Named Georgia Legislative Conservationist of the Year for his support of the Metropolitan Rivers Protection Act of 1974
1976 (Jan)	Serves on the Kennesaw Junior College Board of Trustees, pivotal in getting funds for college to become four-year institution
1976 (Feb)	Campaigns for Carter in the New Hampshire primary
1976 (Mar 31)	Announces he will run for Speaker of the House
1976 (Apr 26)	Cookout for "Al Burruss Appreciation Day"; three thousand five hundred people attend
1976 (Nov 11)	Loses the race for Speaker of the House to Tom Murphy
1980 (Nov 4)	Elected majority whip in House
1982	Elected House majority leader, a post held until his death
1984	Named Cobb County Citizen of the Year
1986 (Mar 9)	Announces he has pancreatic cancer
1986 (Mar 19)	City of Marietta announces the new forty-six-acre park under construction to be named the A. L. Burruss Nature Park
1986 (Mar 27)	Delivers Lenten Lunch Lift speech to First United Methodist Church of Marietta from his hospital bed (tape-recorded)
1986 (May 10)	Dies at Kennestone Hospital, Marietta, Georgia

1987 (Jan 20)	Dedication of the new Burruss Correctional Training Center in Monroe County
1987 (Feb 9)	Plans announced for A. L. Burruss Institute of Public Service & Research at Kennesaw State University
1988 (Jul)	Board of Regents of the University System of Georgia create the A. L. Burruss Institute of Public Service & Research
1988	Dedication of the new A. L. Burruss Elementary School in Marietta, Georgia

Appendix A

Transcript of A. L. Burruss Lenten Lunch Lift Speech,

March 26, 1986

INT: This is Al Burruss speaking for the Lenten Lunch Lift at First United Methodist Church in Marietta, Georgia, on March 26, 1986, from his hospital bed at Kennestone Hospital where he's recovering from exploratory surgery.

Al Burruss: My medical condition prevents me from being with you in person today. When Charles [Rev. Charles Sineath] called me several weeks ago about making this talk I decided I would stress to you that my basic religious beliefs are contained in the Apostle's Creed. I plan to talk with you about God being the only God, our Father Almighty, the Maker of Heaven and Earth. And then I wanted to talk with you about how I believe in Jesus Christ, God's only son, our Savior, our Lord and our Redeemer, who the Bible tells us was born of the Virgin Mary, suffered under Pontius Pilate and was crucified on the cross for the atonement of the sins, of not only you, but of me. Yes, he died and was buried in the tomb. Then I wanted to talk with you about the Resurrection. Remember that without the Resurrection, all other things we believe about God, that we believe about Jesus Christ, that we believe about the Holy Spirit are really not important because our life here on Earth is horrible. Our eternal life comes about through the Resurrection of Christ. This is the ultimate goal that we all seek. I am convinced that I believe these things very strongly. That the events that have occurred during the last few days have emphasized that my beliefs are really stronger than I thought. Since the news has come that I have pancreatic cancer that is most probably terminal, I've been strangely calm and sustained. I give all the credit for this to the fact that my faith was there stronger than even I believed it to be. I am not panicked. It's true that I have spoken about the possibility that my life will be shorter than I want it to be. But I am also encouraged by the fact that my faith tells me that my death and my judgment days can be changed, but they can only be changed by our God and our Maker. Because of my prayers, the prayers of my family and the prayers of so many of you here, and other people throughout this county and throughout this great state of Georgia, I feel there has been an intervention and it is now to have complete or partial healing take place. This is the direct result of prayers for my spiritual and physical improvement. Please take this message home with you: God is real and He will be with us through any trial or tribulation that may come our way. I firmly believe that God is greater than any problems that we have. Please continue to remember to pray for me and my family. I thank you for listening and may God bless you.

APPENDIX B

A. L. BURRUSS INSTITUTE OF PUBLIC SERVICE & RESEARCH

In July 1988, the Georgia Board of Regents of the University System of Georgia created the A. L. Burruss Institute of Public Service & Research. Its mission "is to enhance the ability of governmental agencies and non-profit organizations to make informed decisions for the public good by providing relevant data, technical resources and skill development."

President Betty L. Siegel with Bobbi Burruss at the Founding Ceremony for the A. L. Burruss Institute of Public Service & Research. (1988)

To accomplish this mission in line with Kennesaw State University President Betty L. Siegel's goal of "commitment to community," the Institute made plans to reach out to city, county, regional, state, and federal agencies and elected officials, as well as non-profit and community service organizations. It aimed to provide technical assistance and applied research services on diverse topics ranging from gerontology to lake management studies within North Atlanta and Northwest Georgia.

The A. L. Burruss Institute of Public Service & Research draws upon the expertise of the academic departments of Kennesaw State by providing opportunities for many faculty, from diverse research fields, to participate in applied research projects on an as-needed basis. In addition, Kennesaw State University students serve as student assistants, interns, co-ops, and as interviewers in the Institute's Telephone Survey Research Laboratory. Moreover, the Institute's staff also has extensive community involvement of its own, taking part in many voluntary programs with government agencies, the juvenile court system, chambers of commerce and civic organizations, often speaking to these groups, advising them and sharing in their enterprises.

Since its inception in 1988, the Institute has partnered with a number of prominent organizations, including the Army Corps of Engineers, the Lake Allatoona Watershed Study, and the Nature Conservancy, and it has collaborated on joint projects with other universities, including Emory University and the University of Georgia. The Institute also assists many local, state, and national government agencies, such as the Department of Justice, the Governor's Office of Highway Safety, and other law enforcement departments.

NOTES FOR CHAPTER 1

1. See Ross Bodle, "Burruss Cites Power of Faith in Taped Message to Group," *The Marietta Daily Journal (MDJ)* 26 Mar. 1986, 1 A.
2. In 1964, Cobb County voters ushered in a new form of county government when it voted to move from a single county commissioner, an office long held by Herbert C. McCollum, to a five-member county commission. For an in-depth discussion of this change in Cobb County government, see Thomas Allan Scott's excellent study of everything relating to Cobb County history, *Cobb County, Georgia and the Origins of the Suburban South: A Twentieth-Century History* (Marietta: Cobb Landmarks & Historical Society, 2003).
3. Governor Roy E. Barnes, interview by author, tape recording, Marietta, GA, 12 Dec. 2006.
4. See Tom Bennett, "Al Burruss, Majority Leader of State House, Dies at 58," *The Atlanta Journal and Constitution (AJC)* 11 May 1986, 1 A.
5. *A. L. Burruss: A Remembrance*, prod. Peter Kolstad and Rick Westaway, 45 min., Georgia Public Television and Kennesaw State College, GPB-TV, Atlanta, 1992, videocassette.
6. Born 5 June 1905, in Forsyth County, GA, the son of L. Z. Burruss and Sarah I. Brooks, both born in Forsyth County, GA.
7. Born 22 Jan. 1908, in Forsyth County, GA, the daughter of Alfred L. Corn, born 30 Jan. 1867 in Dawson County, GA (died 16 April 1943 in Forsyth County, GA), and Sarah Cardine Grogan, born 23 April 1871 in Dawson County, GA (died 17 March 1941 in Forsyth County, GA). Burruss's parents were married 26 Sept. 1926 in Forsyth County, GA.
8. Bobbi Burruss and Reneé Burruss Davis, interview by author, tape recording, Marietta, GA, 22 June 2006.
9. Burruss and Davis, interview.
10. Linda Burruss Moore, telephone conversation with author, 25 May 2007.
11. See Celestine Sibley, "Speaker Pro Tem Burruss Worked Hard to Get There," *AJC* 27 Jan. 1974, 11A.
12. *ibid.*
13. *ibid.*
14. Chet Austin, interview by author, tape recording, Marietta, GA, 27 June 2006.
15. Re-Elect Al Burruss: A Champion Legislator for Cobb County, Friends for Al Burruss, campaign brochure, 1984.
16. Sibley, "Speaker Pro Tem."
17. Austin, interview.
18. *ibid.*
19. Jane Burruss Ragan, telephone conversation with author, 29 May 2007.
20. Sibley, "Speaker Pro Tem."
21. Austin, interview.
22. *ibid.*
23. Sibley, "Speaker Pro Tem."
24. Austin, interview.

25. *ibid.*
26. Bobbi Burruss was born 18 Sept. 1931 in Habersham County, Georgia, the daughter of Eugene Elrod, Sr. (1895–1951) and Jessie Mae Robinson (1902–1993).
27. Burruss and Davis interview.
28. *ibid.*
29. This information was found in the Biographical Questionnaire for Permanent Preservation in the Georgia Department of Archives and History, H. R. District 117, for A. L. Burruss, 10 Mar. 1972, Georgia Archives, Morrow, GA.
30. Austin, interview.
31. See Scott, *Cobb County*, note 18, p. 820.
32. Smyrna Historical and Geneological Society. "History of Smyrna." http://www.smyrnahistory.org/_history_ofsmyrna.htm 2006 (accessed May 25, 2007). According to this website, Smyrna's population in early 2006 was estimated at fifty thousand.
33. Austin, interview.
34. Barnes, interview.
35. Austin, interview.
36. Re-Elect Al Burruss.
37. Rev. Charles Sineath, interview by author, tape recording, Bent Tree, GA, 7 August 2006.
38. Rev. Sineath, interview.
39. A. L. Burruss, Lenten Lunch Lift, audiotape of speech, 26 March 1986, Marietta, GA. This recording was made from Burruss's hospital bed at Kennestone Hospital, where he was recovering from exploratory surgery. See Appendix A for the transcript of this recording.
40. See Ann Green, "Gratefulness Given for Mothers," *MDJ* 12 May 1985, n.p.
41. Sibley, "Speaker Pro Tem."

NOTES FOR CHAPTER 2

1. Chet Austin, interview by author, tape recording, Marietta, GA, 27 June 2006.
2. See Celestine Sibley, "Legislative Spotlight: Speaker Pro Tem Burruss Worked Hard to Get There," *AJC* 27 Jan. 1974, p. 11B.
3. Austin, interview.
4. *ibid.*
5. Sibley, "Legislative Spotlight."
6. "Women's Voters' Questionnaire: Legislative Candidates Give Views," *MDJ* 8 Sept. 1968, p. 9B.
7. "Jaycees Name A. L. Burruss as Area Young Man of Year," *MDJ* 25 January 1963, p. 1.
8. *ibid.*
9. *ibid.*
10. Phil Garner contended Burruss smoked four packs a day (See "How a Housewife and a Stewardess Saved the Nonsmokers' Bill," 6 April 1975, p. 8-10, p. 26), while Bill Kinney reported Burruss only smoked two packs a day ("This and That," *MDJ* May 16, 1975). Burruss himself acknowledged his heavy smoking habit but without specifying how many packs a day he smoked.
11. Robin Burruss, interview by author, tape recording, Marietta, GA, 6 July 2006.
12. See Thomas Allan Scott. Cobb County, *Georgia and the Origins of the Suburban South: A Twentieth-Century History*, Marietta, GA: Cobb Landmarks & Historical Society, 2003, p. 387.
13. *ibid.*, p. 387.
14. *ibid.*, p. 388.
15. *ibid.*, p. 388.
16. Ad for Cobb County commissioner, Western District, 1964, *MDJ* 11 August 1964, p. 3.
17. Ad for Cobb County commissioner, Western District, 1964, *MDJ* 8 September 1964, p. 17.
18. Ads for Cobb County commissioner, Western District, 1964, *MDJ*. The "AL Burruss Makes One Promise" ad ran a few times, beginning in August 21, 1964. The "Burruss Not Elected!" ad ran several times in the final week of the county commissioner race, beginning October 25, 1964.
19. Tom Scott, "Critique of A. L. Burruss Biography," to the author, 11 Aug. 2007.
20. See Scott, *Cobb County*, pp. 393-94.
21. See John Smyly, "Commission Races: Ingram, Brown, Burruss Win," *MDJ* 4 November 1964, p. 1.
22. Scott, *Cobb County*, p. 397.
23. See Selby McCash, "Commission Splits on Hiring Attorney," *MDJ* 13 Jan. 1965, p. 1.
24. Scott, *Cobb County*, p. 450.
25. "Burruss Will Not Seek Second Term," *MDJ* April 7, 1968, p. 2.
26. *ibid.*
27. "Scramble Seen for Vacated Assembly Seats," *MDJ* Mar. 15, 1968. n.p.
28. Austin, interview.

29. *A. L. Burruss: A Remembrance*, prod. Peter Kolstad and Rick Westaway, 45 min., Georgia Public Television and Kennesaw State College, GPB-TV, Atlanta, 1992, videocassette.
30. Gary M. Fink. "Jimmy Carter (b. 1924)." New Georgia Encyclopedia Online. http://www.georgiaencyclopedia.org/nge/Article.jsp?id=h-676 (accessed October 14, 2006).
31. See "Burruss May Seek State Senate Post," *MDJ* 7 Mar. 1968, p. 1. An article appearing in *The Marietta Daily Journal* on March 15, 1968, also relayed the information that Burruss was considering a run for the senate; see "Scramble Seen for Vacated Assembly Seats," *MDJ* 15 Mar. 1968, p. 1.
32. *ibid*.
33. See "Burruss Will Not Seek Second Term," *MDJ* 7 April 1968, p. 2.
34. *ibid*
35. *ibid*.
36. Austin, interview.
37. "Women Voters' Questionnaire: Legislative Candidates Give Views," *MDJ* 8 Sept. 1968, p. 9B.
38. *ibid*.
39. See Scott, *Cobb County*, pp. 432-433.
40. See Dick West, "Burruss: Proven Caliber," *MDJ* 5 Sept.1968. p. 4.
41. *ibid*.
42. See Bill Schemmel, "Leggett Defeated in Bid for Senate," *MDJ* 27 Sept. 1968, p. 1.
43. See Bill Schemmel, "Court May Pick Post 7 Winner," *MDJ* 13 Sept.1968, p. 1.
44. See Bill Schemmel, "Leggett to File Suit for Recount," *MDJ* 16 Sept.1968, p. 1.
45. See "'Long Count' Unnecessary," *MDJ* 18 Sept. 1968, p. 4.
46. See "Leggett Reduces Gap on Burruss," *MDJ* 22 Sept. 1968. p. 1.
47. See Bill Schemmel, "Leggett Defeated in Bid for Senate," *MDJ* 27 Sept.1968, p. 1.
48. See Bill Schemmel, "All Cobb Demos Triumph," *MDJ* 5 Nov. 1968, p. 1.
49. Ad for Democratic Ticket, November election. *MDJ* Nov. 3, 1968, p. 9B.
50. See Bill Schemmel, "New Faces Dot Cobb Delegation to Legislature," *MDJ* 12 Jan.1969, p. 2.
51. See Bill Schemmel, "Delegation Dislikes Tax Bills," *MDJ* 24 Feb.1969, p. 1.
52. See Bill Schemmel, "Cobb Legislators Rap Tax Group's Inaction; Wilson: Wasted People's Money," *MDJ* 11 Dec. 1968. p. 1.
53. See Jerry Duke, "Legislators Rip 'Unfair' Juvenile Home Funding," *MDJ* 27 Dec. 1968, p. 1.
54. See "Gas Tax Hike OK Foreseen by Legislators," *MDJ* 9 Jan. 1969. p. 1.
55. See "Redistricting Tops Cobb Assembly Bills," *MDJ* 12 Jan. 1969, p. 1.
56. *ibid*.
57. See "Burruss Heads Attempt to Cut Savings Time," *MDJ* 22 Jan. 1969, p. 1.
58. See Bill Schemmel, "Delegation Dislikes Tax Bills," *MDJ* 24 Feb. 1969, p. 1.
59. See Bill Schemmel, "Cobb Forces Help Kill 'Weed' Tax," *MDJ* 6 Mar. 1969, p. 1.
60. Schemmel, "Delegation."

NOTES FOR CHAPTER 3

1. *A. L. Burruss: A Remembrance,* prod. Peter Kolstad and Rick Westaway, 45 min., Georgia Public Television and Kennesaw State College, GPB-TV, Atlanta, 1992, videocassette.
2. ibid.
3. ibid.
4. See Gary M. Fink, *Prelude to the Presidency: The Political Character and Legislative Leadership Style of Governor Jimmy Carter,* Westport, CT: Greenwood Press, 1980, pp. 164-65.
5. See Fink; Leslie Wheeler, *Jimmy Who?: An Examination of Presidential Candidate Jimmy Carter: The Man, His Career, His Stands on the Issues.* Woodbury, NY: Barron's, 1976; and Martin Schram, *Running for President: A Journal of the Carter Campaign,* NY: Pocket Books, 1976. These authors examine Carter's gubernatorial record.
6. *A. L. Burruss: A Remembrance.*
7. Terry Lawler, interview by author, tape recording, Atlanta, GA, 1 Dec. 2006.
8. *A. L. Burruss: A Remembrance.*
9. Fink, pp. 148-49.
10. Wheeler, p. 70.
11. Quoted in Fink, p. 169.
12. See Frederick Burger, "Speaker's Death Rocks Assembly," *MDJ* 10 Dec.1973, p. 1.
13. See "Will Not Be a Candidate for Speaker, Says Busbee," *AJC* 13 Dec. 1973, p. 1A.
14. See Horell Raines, "Murphy Vows He Will Be Speaker," *AJC* 14 Dec. 1973. p. 16.
15. See Frederick Burger, "Al Burruss Frontrunner for House Post," *MDJ* 14 Dec. 1973, p. 8.
16. ibid.
17. ibid.
18. See Celestine Sibley, "Speaker Pro Tem Burruss Worked Hard to Get There," *AJC* 27 January 1974. p. 11.
19. ibid.
20. ibid.
21. ibid.
22. See Frederick Burger, "Burruss Elected," *MDJ* 7 January 1974, p. 2.
23. See Milo Dakin, "Rep. Burruss Nominated," *AJC* 8 January 1974, p. 2.
24. See "Burruss Confirmed as Speaker Pro Tem," *MDJ* 14 Jan. 1974, p. 2.
25. Tom Scott, "Critique of A. L. Burruss Biography," 11 August 2007. See also "Blue Law: At Last Some Kind of Relief," *MDJ* 8 Feb. 1974, p. 4.
26. See Frederick Burger, "Women's Credit Bill Approved," *MDJ* 1 Feb. 1974, p. 1.
27. ibid.
28. Lawler, interview.
29. See David Morrison, "No Smoking Bill Passes," *AJC* 1 March 1975, p. A3.
30. ibid.
31. See *Major Environmental Laws.* Georgia Center for Law in the Public Interest. http://www.cleangeorgia.org/net/content/page.aspx?s=19578.0.1.19069 (accessed 20 July 2007).
32. See "The Georgia Wildlife Federation Presents Conservation Awards to Seventeen Georgians, Two Groups," *Georgia Outdoors* May 1975, pp. 5, 12.

33. ibid.
34. Jane Ragan, telephone conversation with author, 29 May 2007.
35. See Thomas Allan Scott, *Cobb County, Georgia and the Origins of the Suburban South: A Twentieth-Century History*, Marietta, GA: Cobb Landmarks & Historical Society, 2003, p. 430. Some of this information was also related in an interview by the author with Tom Scott, tape recording, Kennesaw, GA, 8 June 2006.
36. Tom Scott, interview by author, tape recording, Kennesaw, GA, 8 June 2006.
37. Thomas A. Scott. "Kennesaw State University." The New Georgia Encyclopedia Online. http://www.georgiaencyclopedia.org/nge/Article.jsp?id=h-852&pid=s-60 (accessed August 19, 2005).
38. *ibid.*
39. *ibid.*
40. See Rick Beene, "Panel to Mark Funds for KJC," *MDJ* 30 Jan. 1976, p. 1.
41. See Rick Beene, "Al Burruss–Cobb's Legislative Ace," *MDJ* 7 March 1976, p. 1.
42. *ibid.*
43. See Frederick Burger, "Bill Drawn to Aid STI Students," *MDJ* 27 Feb. 1975, p. 8.
44. See Frederick Burger, "Assembly Split Over Sunshine," *MDJ* 13 Jan. 1975, p. 1. However, a compromise was later reached, allowing both the House and Senate to vote to close a session if work could not be done under public scrutiny (see Rex Granum, "'Sunshine' Ruling for Panels Gaining," *AJC* 29 Jan. 1975, p. 1A).
45. Gov. Roy E. Barnes, interview by author, tape recording, Marietta, GA, 12 Dec. 2006.
46. See Arnold Fleischmann and Carol Pierannunzi, *Politics in Georgia*, Athens: University of Georgia Press, 1997, p. 149. Fleischmann and Pierannunzi describe the "broad powers" of the Speaker of the House, including "the ability to change the order of bills appearing on the calendar and to control floor debate through recognition of members, suspension of debate, and decisions about the appropriateness of amendments.... In addition, the Speaker is second in line to succeed the governor after the lieutenant governor."
47. See Fleischmann and Pierannunzi, p. 149.
48. *ibid.*
49. Press Release. Remarks of Rep. Al Burruss, Speaker Pro Tem, Marietta for Release at 10 AM 31 March 1976.
50. See Joe Brown, "Burruss Runs for Speaker," *AJC* 1 Apr. 1976, p. 14 A.
51. See "Burruss: A Drive for House Reform," *MDJ* 8 Apr. 1976, p. 4.
52. *A. L. Burruss: A Remembrance.*
53. See Sharon Salyer, "Mr. Speaker: Murphy Keeps Reins," *MDJ* 11 Nov. 1976, p. 1.
54. See Rick Beene, "Burruss Accepts Loss," *MDJ* 11 Nov. 1976, p. 1.
55. See "Object Lesson," *AJC* 7 Dec.1976, p. 4.
56. *A. L. Burruss: A Remembrance.*
57. *ibid.*
58. See Fleischmann and Pierannunzi, p. 173.
59. *A. L. Burruss: A Remembrance.*

NOTES FOR CHAPTER 4

1. Tom Scott, interview by author, tape recording, Kennesaw, GA, 8 June 2006.
2. See Arnold Fleischmann and Carol Pierannunzi, *Politics in Georgia*, Athens: University of Georgia Press, 1997, p. 173.
3. ibid.
4. *A. L. Burruss: A Remembrance,* prod. Peter Kolstad and Rick Westaway, 45 min., Georgia Public Television and Kennesaw State College, GPB-TV, Atlanta, 1992, videocassette.
5. Chet Austin, interview by author, tape recording, Marietta, GA, 27 June 2006.
6. Legislative aide, anonymous, interview by author, tape recording, Acworth, GA, 31 October 2006. She was a legislative aide and research analyst during her long career at the House and served on the Ways and Means Committee for twenty-seven years. She knew Marcus Collins and Al Burruss very well.
7. ibid.
8. ibid.
9. ibid.
10. ibid.
11. Pete Phillips's speech at the Democratic caucus in November, 1980; read to author by legislative aide, anonymous, during her interview with the author, tape recording, Acworth, GA, 31 Oct. 2006.
12. *A. L. Burruss: A Remembrance.*
13. ibid
14. Legislative aide, anonymous, interview. She expressly asked not to be identified in the book's text, and therefore appears as the "long-time legislative aide on the Ways and Means Committee."
15. ibid. After Burruss's death, she was given this jar of ointment with the fly in it and still has it in her possession.
16. Governor Roy E. Barnes, interview by author, tape recording, Marietta, GA, 12 Dec. 2006.
17. Legislative aide, interview.
18. *A. L. Burruss: A Remembrance.*
19. Barnes, interview.
20. Pete Phillips's speech at the Democratic caucus in November, 1980.
21. Legislative aide, interview.
22. *A. L. Burruss: A Remembrance.*
23. Barnes, interview.
24. See Hal Straus, "Making the Big Plays: 10 Men to Watch: Little Fanfare, but a Lot of Clout," *AJC* 1 Jan.1985. p. 12.
25. See Frederick Allen, "What's a GOP Leader to Do?" *AJC* 13 Jan. 1985, p. 1.
26. See Thomas Allan Scott, *Cobb County, Georgia and the Origins of the Suburban South: A Twentieth-Century History*, Marietta, GA: Cobb Landmarks & Historical Society, 2003, p. 474.
27. See Beau Cutts, "Burruss, Nix Race Ends Courteously," *MDJ* 4 November 1970, p. 3C.

28. *ibid.*
29. See Dee Bryant, "3 Key Assembly Posts Claimed by Local GOP," *MDJ* 8 Nov. 1972, p. 1.
30. *ibid.* Hal Suit had won the most votes in Cobb County in the gubernatorial campaign against Jimmy Carter, who would win the election to become governor of Georgia.
31. See Tom Sharp, "Burruss Handily Checks Challenge from Howard," *MDJ* 7 Nov. 1984, p. 5B.
32. *ibid.*
33. See "Election '84: Our Recommendations," *MDJ* 4 Nov. 1984, p. 10B.
34. See "Four House Posts Are Contested in Cobb," *MDJ* 4 Nov. 1984, p. 3B.
35. See Bill Kinney, "Tuesday Will Be Exciting Here," *MDJ* 4 Nov. 1984, p. 10B.
36. *ibid.*
37. See Maggie Willis, "Republicans to Gain Nine Offices," *MDJ* 7 Nov. 1984, p. 10B.
38. See Susan Miller, "Big Cobb Vote Good for GOP," *MDJ* 6 Nov. 1980, p. 1A.
39. *ibid.*
40. Sharp, p. 5B.
41. See Martin Schram, *Running for President: A Journal of the Carter Campaign*, NY: Pocket Books, 1976. p. 21.
42. Gerald Burruss, telephone conversation with author, 27 July 2007.
43. "State Briefings on Panama Canal Treaty. Tuesday, August 30, 1977; 3:45 P.M. (15 minutes); The State Dining Room." Obtained from the Jimmy Carter Library online web request; sent via email by Albert Nason, Archivist, Jimmy Carter Library. Zell Miller, then Georgia's Lieutenant Governor, was also one of the attendees.
44. The Jimmy Carter Library archives.
45. The Jimmy Carter Library archives.
46. The Jimmy Carter Library archives.
47. Gerald Burruss, interview.
48. See "Burruss Plans to Run for Majority Whip Job," *MDJ* 6 Nov. 1980, p. 8A.
49. "Political Roles in the Legislature." http://www.legis.state.ga.us/legis/2007_08/house/kids/whosWho.htm (accessed August 2, 1997).
50. See Brent Gilroy, "Burruss Named to Revision Panel," *MDJ* 14 May 1981, p. 3A.
51. *A. L. Burruss: A Remembrance.*
52. Legislative aide, interview.
53. Fleischmann and Pierannunzi, p. 161.
54. See Dick Pettys, "Things Happen in Assembly When Rep. Murphy Speaks," *Griffin Daily News* 8 Jan.1985, n.p. (Article clip located in Burruss Scrapbook 1985-1986. The A. L. Burruss Institute for Public Service & Research, Kennesaw State University.)
55. "Political Roles in the Legislature."
56. Fleischmann and Pierannunzi, p. 162.
57. *ibid.*
58. Budget Office, Georgia House of Representatives "Georgia Budget Process." http://www.legis.state.ga.us/legis/2007_08/house/budget/budgetProcess.html (accessed August 2, 2007).
59. *A. L. Burruss: A Remembrance.*

60. *ibid.*
61. *ibid.*
62. Legislative aide, interview.
63. *A. L. Burruss: A Remembrance.*
64. *MDJ* 12 Jan. 1985, n.p. Burruss Scrapbook 1985–1986. The A. L. Burruss Institute for Public Service & Research, Kennesaw State University.
65. See Tom Sharp, "Cobb Democrats Are to Introduce Exemption Bill," *MDJ* 15 Jan. 1985, p. 6A.
66. Terry Lawler, interview by author, tape recording, Atlanta, GA, 1 Dec. 2006.
67. See Bill Carbine, "Majority Leader Burruss Focuses on Improving Education," *AJC* 31 Aug. 1983, n.p.
68. *ibid.*
69. *ibid.*
70. See Jane O. Hansen, "Harris Hails Education Report," *AJC* 13 Nov. 1984, p. 1A.
71. *ibid.* See also Tom Sharp, "Legislator Says Teachers Must Be Accountable," *MDJ* 20 Dec. 1984, p. 1A.
72. See Jane Hansen and Prentice Palmer, "What the Legislator Will Face: School Issue, Drinking Reforms Await Lawmakers Next Week," *AJC* 6 Jan. 1985, p. 1A.
73. See Frederick Burger, "Cobb Delegates Get High Marks," *MDJ* 30 Mar. 1975, p. 1A. Burruss was instrumental in getting a compromise for the kindergarten legislation but there was no money to fund it.
74. See Frederick Allen, "Political Sidestep Was Legislators' Favorite Dance," *AJC* 10 Mar. 1985, p. 6B.
75. Barnes, interview. This meeting probably took place in January 1985; Tom Sharp reported in the *MDJ*, "Local 1% tax for Roads to be Introduced Soon," Jan. 16, 1985, p. 1A, that Burruss would be responsible for getting the 1 percent local sales tax option introduced.
76. Barnes, interview.
77. Scott, interview.
78. *A. L. Burruss: A Remembrance.*
79. Barnes, interview.
80. See "Local-Option Sales Tax Bill may Bring More $$ to Cobb," *MDJ* 18 Jan.1986, p. 4A.
81. *A. L. Burruss: A Remembrance.*
82. See "Building Projects Reduced," *MDJ* 6 Feb. 1986, p. 1A.
83. See "Democratic House Members Build War-Chest," *MDJ* 12 Sept. 1985, n.p.
84. *ibid.*
85. Barnes, interview.
86. Lawler, interview.
87. Legislative aide, interview.
88. *ibid.*
89. *ibid.*
90. *A. L. Burruss: A Remembrance.*
91. See Hal Straus, "House Raps Senate for Adjourning: Legislators See Need for Procedural Change," *AJC* 9 Mar. 1986, p. 1A.

NOTES FOR CHAPTER 5

1. See Hank Ezell, "Friends Remember 'Quiet Giver': Burruss Praised for Endless Energy, Compassion and Attention to Detail," *AJC* 11 May 1986, p. 9A.
2. See Tom Bennett, "Al Burruss, Majority Leader of State House, Dies at 58," *AJC* 11 May 1986, 1A.
3. *ibid.*
4. See Merritt Cowart, "Carters Among Those Who Mourn Burruss," *MDJ* 12 May 1986, p. 1.
5. Cowart, "Friends Mourn Burruss," p. 8A.
6. See Salynn Boyles, "Burruss Called 'Giving, Wise' Friend, Leader," *MDJ* 13 May 1986, p. 1.
7. See Bill Kinney, "In Limousines and Pickups, They Came to Honor Burruss," *MDJ* 13 May 1986, p. 1.
8. *ibid.*
9. See Kevin Sack, "Over 1,500 Attend Burruss' Funeral: House Majority Leader is Eulogized as 'Something Special,'" *AJC* 13 May 1986, p. 11A.
10. Kinney, p. 1.
11. Sack, p. 11A.
12. See Salynn Boyles, "Park Is Named for Al Burruss," *MDJ* 19 March 1986, p. 6A.
13. A. L. Burruss, Lenten Lunch Lift, audiotape of speech, 26 March 1986, Marietta, GA. See Appendix A for the complete transcript.
14. Barnes, interview.
15. *MDJ* 5 April 1986, n.p. Burruss Scrapbook 1985–1986. The A. L. Burruss Institute for Public Service & Research, Kennesaw State University.
16. By Tom Bennett's account ("Al Burruss, Majority Leader of State House, Dies at 58"), there were thousands of visitors; a later news report (Ross Bidle, "Burruss Cites Power of Faith in Taped Message to Group," *MDJ* 27 March 1986, p. 1A.) put it at hundreds.
17. Kinney, p. 1.
18. Letter from David C. Evans, commissioner, Georgia Department of Corrections, to Mrs. Chessley [sic] Burruss and Mr. Gerald Burruss. A. L. Burruss 1985–1986 Scrapbook. The A. L. Burruss Institute for Public Service & Research, Kennesaw State University.
19. "Burruss Public Service Institute Planned." Monday Report. A Kennesaw College Publication for Faculty and Staff. Feb. 9, 1987, p. 1. A. L. Burruss 1985–1986 Scrapbook. The A. L. Burruss Institute for Public Service & Research, Kennesaw State University.
20. *ibid.*
21. *A. L. Burruss Institute of Public Service & Research*, retrieved August 4, 2007, http://www.kennesaw.edu/burruss_inst/about/.
22. *A. L. Burruss: A Remembrance,* prod. Peter Kolstad and Rick Westaway, 45 min., Georgia Public Television and Kennesaw State College, GPB-TV, Atlanta, 1992, videocassette.
23. See Merritt Cowart, "Friends Mourn Burruss Loss," *MDJ* 11 May 1986, p. 8A.

SELECT BIBLIOGRAPHY

Anderson, Patrick. *Electing Jimmy Carter: The Campaign of 1976.* Baton Rouge: Louisiana State University Press, 1994.

Bisher, Furman, and Celestine Sibley. *Atlanta's Half-Century: As Seen through the Eyes of Columnists Furman Bisher and Celestine Sibley.* AJC: Longstreet Press, 1997.

Carter, Jimmy. *Turning Point: A Candidate, a State, and a Nation Come of Age.* New York: Three Rivers Press, 1992.

———. *An Hour Before Daylight: Memories of a Rural Boyhood.* New York: Simon & Schuster, 2001.

Cobb, James C. *Georgia Odyssey.* Athens, Ga.: The University of Georgia Press, 1997.

Coleman, Kenneth, ed. *A History of Georgia.* 2nd ed. Athens, Ga.: The University of Georgia Press, 1981.

Eldredge, Richard, ed. *Celestine Sibley, Reporter.* Athens, Ga.: Hill Street Press, 2001.

Fink, Gary M. *Prelude to the Presidency: The Political Character and Legislative Leadership Style of Governor Jimmy Carter.* Westport, Conn.: Greenwood Press, 1980.

Fleischmann, Arnold, and Carol Pierannunzi. *Politics in Georgia.* Athens, Ga.: The University of Georgia Press, 2007.

Fleming, Sibley. *Celestine: A Granddaughter's Reminiscences.* Athens, Ga.: Hill Street Press, 2002.

Henderson, Harold P., and Gary L. Roberts, eds. *Georgia Governors in an Age of Change: From Ellis Arnall to George Busbee.* Athens, Ga.: The University of Georgia Press, 1988.

Saye, Albert B. *Georgia Government and History.* Evanston, Ill.: Row, Peterson, 1957.

Schram, Martin. *Running for President: A Journal of the Carter Campaign.* New York: Pocket Books, 1976.

———. *Running for President 1976: The Carter Campaign.* New York: Stein and Day, 1977.

Scott, Thomas Allan. *Cobb County, Georgia and the Origins of the Suburban South: A Twentieth-Century History.* Marietta, Ga.: Cobb Landmarks & Historical Society, Inc., 2003.

Sibley, Celestine. *The Celestine Sampler: Writings and Photographs with Tributes to the Beloved Author and Journalist.* Atlanta, GA: Peachtree, 1997.

Wheeler, Leslie. *Jimmy Who?: An Examination of Presidential Candidate Jimmy Carter: The Man, His Career, His Stands on the Issues.* Woodbury, N.Y.: Barron's, 1976

INDEX

A

Allen, Frederick 75, 82, 105, 107
Appropriations Committee 6, 37, 70, 72 (*see also* House Appropriations Committee)
Arnall, Ellis 23, 109
Atherton, Howard 28, 30
Atlanta Journal and Constitution, The 3, 67, 74, 79, 99
Austin, Chet ix, xii, 3, 16, 23, 39, 43, 44, 63, 88

B

Banks, E. T. 5, 15
Barnes, Roy E. 2, 38, 66, 67, 72, 73, 75, 77, 78, 81, 83
Barrett, Ernest 21
Bartow County 78
Bell Aircraft 4
Brown, Betty 86
Brown, Tommy 22
Brumby, Otis 89
Burger, Frederick 34, 103, 104, 107
Burruss, A. L.
  as Cobb County Commissioner 29
  as family man 20, 56, 60
  as fiscal conservative 22, 26
  as Gov. Carter's floor man 31, 32, 33, 34, 74, 77, 92
  as legislator 29, 30, 32, 33, 34, 36, 64, 65, 68, 73, 77, 82, 85
  as majority whip 41, 65, 66, 67, 70
  as minority leader 77
  as Speaker pro tempore 34, 39, 40, 63, 67, 84
  on anti-smoking legislation 36
  on Equal Rights Amendment 36
  on women's credit bill 35
Burruss, Bobbi 2, 4, 7, 10, 12, 13, 18, 46, 50, 51, 54, 55, 56, 60, 97
Burruss, Buddy xii, 2, 6, 9
Burruss, Chess (A. L.s father) 52
Burruss, Eula (A. L.'s mother) 10, 52, 86
Burruss, Gerald xii, 86, 108
Burruss, Robin xii, 13, 46, 48, 54, 56, 64, 86
Busbee, George 9, 33, 37, 51, 53, 75, 109

C

Calvary Children's Home 14
campaign ads, for county commissioner 21
Capitol, state of Georgia 13, 34, 66, 78, 86
Carbine, Bill 74, 106
Carter, Hugh 33, 53
Carter, Jimmy xi, 1, 14, 18, 23, 31, 33, 38, 41, 49, 53, 61, 69, 70, 84, 87, 92, 101, 103, 105, 106, 109
Carter, Rosalynn 87
Cauthen, Rev. Hugh 87
Cobb County ix, xi, 1, 9, 16, 17, 19, 20, 21, 22, 23, 25, 27, 28, 29, 32, 35, 37, 38, 67, 69, 73, 75, 76, 78, 83, 84, 86, 87, 91, 92, 99, 100, 101, 102, 104, 105, 106, 107, 109
Collins, Marcus 64, 65, 105
Cornelia, GA 5, 17, 18
county commission ix, 1, 19, 20, 22, 24, 48, 91

D

Dakin, Milo 35, 103
Darden, Buddy 82, 87
Davis, Renée Burruss xii, 2, 5, 11, 12, 18, 46, 52, 54, 55, 56, 61, 86, 91

E

Edwards, Juanelle 68
Equal Rights Amendment (ERA) 35

F

Fink, Gary M. 32, 33, 101, 103, 109
First United Methodist Church of Marietta xii, 7, 75, 87, 92, 95
Fleischmann, Arnold 39, 41, 63, 104, 105, 109
Flournoy, Bob 19, 21
Forsyth County 2, 3, 9, 73, 74, 88, 91, 99
Fowler, Rachel 70

G

General Assembly (state of Georgia) ix, 14, 19, 23, 24, 30, 31, 34, 35, 67, 70, 72, 74, 77, 79, 82
Godwin, Art 18
Green, Vernon 5, 15

H

Haines, Gordon 17
Harris, Joe Frank 6, 37, 54, 74, 78

Henderson, J. H. 29
Hensley, Sam P. 24, 29
Hines, Harris 40, 66, 88
Holloway, Al 33
House Appropriations Committee (state of Georgia) 37, 72
House of Representatives (state of Georgia) (*see also* state legislature; General Assembly, state of Georgia) ix, 1, 23, 31, 32, 40, 92, 106
House Rules Committee (state of Georgia) 70, 71
House Ways and Means Committee (state of Georgia) 64, 65, 77, 105
Housley, Eugene 29
Howard, Doug 68

I

Ingram, Harold 22, 101
Isakson, Johnny 76, 77

J

Jordan, Ben 21

K

Kennesaw State University ix, xi, 31, 77, 93, 98, 104, 106, 108
  as Kennesaw Junior College 37, 92
  as Kennesaw State College 31, 55, 77, 83, 88, 99, 101, 103, 105, 108
Kilgore, Tom 72
Kinney, Bill 68, 84, 86, 101, 105, 108
Knight, Nathan 70
Kreeger Jr., George 28

L

Lawler, Terry xii, 33, 35, 68, 74, 78, 103, 106
Lee, Bill 34
Leggett, Homer 25, 28, 102
legislator (*see also* state legislator) 29, 30, 32, 33, 34, 36, 64, 65, 68, 73, 77, 82, 85

M

Maddox, Lester 23
Marietta Daily Journal, The 10, 20, 22, 24, 25, 28, 30, 34, 40, 68, 77, 84, 86, 87, 89, 99, 101
Marietta High School 11
McCollum, Herbert C. 17, 99
McDaniell, Hugh Lee 29
Metropolitan Atlanta Transit Authority (MARTA) 26

Metropolitan Rivers Protection Act of 1974 36, 92
Miller, Zell 85, 87, 106
Moore, Linda (Burruss) xii, 3, 10
Mount Zion United Methodist Church 87
Murphy, Tom 34, 35, 38, 40, 41, 61, 64, 66, 67, 83, 87, 92

N

Nix, Ken 67
Nixon, Richard 28

O

Oliver, Bill 21

P

Panama Canal, Treaty of 70, 106
pancreatic cancer 8, 31, 79, 81, 86, 87, 92, 95
Paulding County 23, 25, 28, 36, 78, 82
Peanut Brigade 69
Philippines 4, 9, 15, 91
Phillips, Pete 65
Pierannunzi, Carol xi, 39, 41, 63, 71, 104, 105, 106, 109
politics ix, 1, 2, 13, 15, 19, 24, 40, 67, 72, 78, 84, 89
Politics in Georgia 63, 104, 105, 109
Porter, DuBose 63
Prelude to the Presidency 32, 103, 109

Q

Quality Basic Education 74

R

Ragan, Jane Burruss xii, 2, 9, 99, 103
Rainwater, Betty 70
Reagan, Ronald 69
Richardson, Eleanor 73, 79
Rules Committee (*see also* House Rules Committee) 70, 71

S

sales tax 27, 30, 75, 76, 107
sales tax, local option 30, 75, 76
Schemmel, Bill 30, 102
Scott, Thomas Allan xi, 99, 101, 103, 105
Sharp, Tom 68, 106, 107

Shepard, Neal 70
Shields, Paul 31, 63, 76
Shipp, Bill 38, 77
Sibley, Celestine 3, 12, 34, 36, 99, 101, 103, 109
Siegel, Betty 89, 97
Simpson, George 37
Sineath, Rev. Charles xii, 7, 81, 85, 87, 95, 100
Smith, George L., II 33
Smyrna, GA 3, 4, 5, 7, 14, 15, 20, 74, 91, 100
Smyrna High School 4, 91
Southern Polytechnic State University, (*see also* Southern Tech) 17
Southern Tech 38, 77
Speaker, of the House of Representatives 39, 41, 92, 104
Speaker pro tempore 34, 39, 40, 63, 67, 84
SPLOST 76
state legislator 29, 33
state legislature 11, 14, 25, 84
state representative (*see also* state legislator) vii, 31, 72, 73, 76
Straus, Hal 67, 105, 107
Sunshine Law 38
Sutton, Frank 33

T

Thompson, Steve 32
Tillman Memorial Methodist Church 7, 20
Tip Top Poultry, Inc. ix, 1, 5, 6, 9, 14, 16, 17, 20, 39, 82, 86, 91

U

Urban Renewal Program 16
US Naval Reserve 15

W

Ways and Means Committee, (*see also* House Ways and Means Committee) 64, 65, 70, 71, 77, 105
West, Dick 27, 102
Western Marietta Little League 11
White House 69, 70
Wilder, Tom 68
Willingham, Harold 37, 38
Wilson, Joe Mack ix, 19, 29, 30, 37, 38, 53, 65, 68, 73, 75, 76, 77, 78, 89

A. L. Burruss 1927–1986

CPSIA information can be obtained at www.ICGtesting.com
Printed in the USA
240961LV00003B/8/P